ADMINISTRATION

publicity

& FUNDRAISING

THE *ideas*
LIBRARY

FOR YOUTH GROUPS

THE IDEAS LIBRARY

ADMINISTRATION
publicity
& FUNDRAISING

THE ideas LIBRARY

FOR YOUTH GROUPS

Youth Specialties

ZondervanPublishingHouse
Grand Rapids, Michigan
A Division of HarperCollinsPublishers

Administration, Publicity, & Fundraising for Youth Groups
Copyright © 1997 by Youth Specialties, Inc.
Youth Specialties Books, 1224 Greenfield Dr., El Cajon, CA 92021, are published by Zondervan Publishing House,
5300 Patterson Ave. SE, Grand Rapids, MI 49530.

Project editor: Vicki Newby
Cover design: Curt Sell
Interior design: Curt Sell and PAZ Design Group
Art director: Mark Rayburn

Printed in the United States of America

ISBN 0-310-22039-4

00 01 02 03 04 05 06 / / 10 9 8 7 6

CONTENTS

101378

So what organizational, promotional, or fundraising trick did wonders for your ministry lately?

Youth Specialties pays $25 (and in some cases, more) for unpublished, field-tested ideas that have worked for you.

You've probably been in youth work long enough to realize that sanitary, theoretical, *tidy* ideas aren't what in-the-trenches youth workers are looking for. They want—*you* want—imagination and take-'em-by-surprise novelty in parties and other events. Ideas that have been tested and tempered and improved in the very real, very adolescent world you work in.

So here's what to do:

• Sit down at your computer, get your killer idea out of your head and onto your hard drive, then e-mail it to ideas@youthspecialties.com. Or print it off and fax it to 619-440-4939 (Attn: Ideas).

• If you need to include diagrams, photos, art, or samples that help explain your idea, stick it all in an envelope and mail it to our street address: Ideas, 1224 Greenfield Dr., El Cajon, CA 92021-3399.

• Be sure to include your name and all your addresses and numbers.

• Let us have about three months to give your idea a thumbs up or down*, and a little longer for your 25 bucks.

*Hey, no offense intended if your idea isn't accepted. It's just that our fussy Ideas Library editor has these *really* meticulous standards. If the idea isn't creative, original, and just plain fun in an utterly wild or delightful way, she'll reject it (reluctantly, though, because she has a tender heart). Sorry. But we figure you deserve only the best ideas.

ALPHABETICAL LIST
OF EVERY IDEA IN THIS BOOK

No one wants to get bogged down in the mundane tasks of youth ministry. But, alas, they're necessary. Here are some tips, time savers, and tricks of the trade to help make you more efficient and more organized when it comes to office work, records, and communication. You'll find advice on everything from creating a personalized reference file to ways of presenting group rules memorably and effectively.

PLANNING, EVALUATION, & RECORD-KEEPING

INFORMATION OVERLOAD

It's important to keep good records on your students and visitors. Here are a few questionnaires to help collect information—choose the one that best suits your needs.

• **Welcome! Glad You're Here!** Use the information form on page 14 for visitors who come to Sunday school, to the midweek meeting, or to special events as a way to let them know you're interested in getting to know them.

• **Form 1040Z.** The questionnaire on page 15 is especially appropriate around tax time.

• **Fun Fact Sheet.** Have kids fill out the form on page 16 for your information and for your use in planning. It also works as a visitor's registration form.

• **Junior High Questionnaire.** The "Hey, welcome to the best years of your life!" questionnaire on page 17 is especially for junior high kids—a sheet that's fun to fill out as well as informative for your leadership team.

• **Youth Group Application for Admission** On pages 18-19 is a fun way to collect vital statistics on your youth group members. It's also a great way to test your kids' sense of humor. Make your application look official. Have all your kids fill it out. Give one to new kids as they come.

There are lots more questionnaires, to spark discussion or to elicit information in *Incredible Questionnaires for Youth Groups* by Rick Bundschuh and E.G. Von Trutzschler, published by Youth Specialties/Zondervan. *Tim Laycock, Byron D. Harvey, Michael Maples, Len Cuthbert, and Tony Liston*

FILE CARDS

You may prefer to keep your records in a card file. This is a helpful way to keep up to date and it provides a good bridge between youth directors, who tend to change frequently. Your file should be compact, yet comprehensive—a 5x7 file is usually sufficient. You may want to keep tabs on the following information:

1. Name, home address, email address, phone number, fax number, age, school, grade, major (if in college).

2. Parents' names, names of brothers and sisters, who live with the student, who are church members.

Welcome!
Glad You're Here!

This information will be used to drive you crazy with phone calls, personal visits, and will be sold to all junk mailers in the world. Just kidding! Actually, this information simply helps us get to know you better.

Name: _____

Address: _____

Phone: _____ Age: _____

School: _____
❑ Jr. High   ❑ Sr. High
❑ Male   ❑ Female

How you came:
❑ Motor boat
❑ Space shuttle
❑ Plane
❑ On a camel
❑ My parents are visiting the church
❑ A friend brought me. If so, who?

_____

Do you attend another church youth group?
❑ Yes   ❑ No

If yes, which one?

_____

Why you came:
❑ My parents dragged me here
❑ I dragged my parents here
❑ I got lost on my way to the movies
❑ I heard this was a great youth group
❑ I'm just visiting—leave me alone

Miscellaneous:
Would you like to be a kidney donor?
❑ Yes   ❑ No
Do you have a dog named Spot?
❑ Yes   ❑ No
Do you think this is a great youth group?
❑ Yes   ❑ Yes
Are you looking for a new youth group?
❑ Yes   ❑ No
Did Adam and Eve have belly buttons?
❑ Yes   ❑ No
Would you like to be put on our mailing list?
❑ Yes, definitely
❑ No, but thanks for the great offer—you people are really special, fantastic, great, wonderful, etc.
❑ I'd like to know more about the youth group—please give me a phone call

FORM 1040z*

NAME	BIRTH DATE AGE
ADDRESS	TELEPHONE
CITY,	STATE, ZIP
SCHOOL	GRADE
SOCIAL SECURITY #	SERIAL # CEREAL

IN YOUR UNDERSTANDING, WHAT DOES A PERSON NEED TO DO TO BECOME A CHRISTIAN?	ITEMIZE YOUR THREE FAVORITE MUSICAL GROUPS OR SINGERS HERE

HAVE YOU EVER BECOME A CHRISTIAN? ....YES . . . . .NO

HAVE YOU BEEN BAPTIZED?...YES . . . . .NO

HAVE YOU HEARD THE ONE ABOUT BOB? ....YES . . . . .NO

HOW'D YOU LIKE A SOCK IN THE NOSE? ....YES . . . . .NO

I HAVE TALENTS IN THE FOLLOWING AREAS:	DO NOTHING HERE
MUSIC WRITING OTHER: PUPPETRY SPORTS DRAMA DRAWING COOKING SNEEZING	

WOULD YOU LIKE TO GIVE A BUCK TO THE PRESIDENTIAL CAMPAIGN OF RONALD McDONALD? ☐ YES ☐ NO ☐ HUH?	I ESPECIALLY HAVE ENJOYED THESE ACTIVITIES IN THE PAST:
I SOLEMNLY SWEAR THAT THESE ANSWERS ARE AT LEAST FAIRLY CLOSE TO ACCURATE...MAYBE.	SIGN HERE, DUMMY

*Z IS FOR ZANY

15

FUN FACT SHEET
WELCOME!

Name _____

Address _____

City _____ Zip _____

School _____ Year _____

Phone Number _____

☐ I would like to know more about this group's activities.
☐ I would like to know more about your Bible studies.
☐ I came with a friend.
☐ I came with my family.
☐ I came on my own.
☐ I came because my parents made me.
☐ I came by accident.
☐ I work at _____
☐ I don't work, but wish I did.
☐ I don't work, and hope I never will.
☐ At school I'm involved in _____
☐ I attend church _____
   ☐ often
   ☐ never
   ☐ now and then
☐ I most often attend church at _____

I like—

☐ Water-skiing
☐ Snowmaking
☐ Reading
☐ Drama
☐ Basketball
☐ Volleyball
☐ Soccer
☐ Football
☐ Chess
☐ Skateboarding
☐ Running
☐ Looking at the opposite sex

☐ Eating
☐ Snowmobiling
☐ Listening to music
☐ Writing on bathroom walls
☐ Reading bathroom walls
☐ Working on cars
☐ Baseball
☐ Frisbee
☐ Sewing
☐ Painting
☐ Driving crazy
☐ Backpacking
☐ Rock climbing

☐ Hanging around and being cool
☐ Picking my nose
☐ Picking my friend's nose
☐ Getting straight A's
☐ Spitting on people who get straight A's
☐ Tennis
☐ Swimming
☐ Surfing
☐ Rollerskating
☐ Golfing
☐ Filling out long questionnaires

Hey, welcome to the best years of your life!

Tell us about yourself!

But first, let us tell you about something we think you'll like:

Okay, now for the questions. Answer them the best you can.

1. So what's your name, anyway? (Easy so far, huh?)_____

2. Birth date (okay, so you may not remember the event, but you know the date—you were there when it happened...)_____

3. How old were you when you were born?____

4. What clubs, teams, or organizations do you belong to? _____

5. Got a favorite sport? (check one box and complete that line)

☐ Yes—and it's _____

☐ Yes—more than one, in fact. My top two are _____

☐ Not especially. Sports are okay, but I have no big favorites.

☐ Are you kidding? Give me a break—I can't stand sports. I'd rather eat sand.

6. All right, all right, enough of sports. Ever taken any music lessons? Play an instrument?
_____

7. What in your life have you done that you still remember as the best moment ever (or almost the best)? _____

8. What would make you want to bring a friend to an event? _____
_____

9. How long have you been coming to this church? Or is this your first time? _____

10. Draw a portrait of yourself.

11. What do you like best about your portrait?

_____
_____

Whoops, time for the religious questions (hey, this is a church, after all). There are no correct answers—really. Any No's or I Don't Knows you check are as acceptable as Yes's—as long as you're honest.

12. Do you believe in God?

☐ Yes   ☐ No   ☐ Not sure

13. Which of these words describe what God is like to you?

☐ Grandfather   ☐ Parent

☐ Boss   ☐ Teacher

☐ Sheriff   ☐ Revolutionary

☐ Your personal servant

14. Do you believe in Jesus Christ?

☐ Yes   ☐ No   ☐ Not sure

15. Do you believe there's a heaven and a hell?

☐ Ye   ☐ No   ☐ Not sure

16. You may not think about this much, but here goes: When you die, where do you think you'll go?

☐ Heaven   ☐ Hell   ☐ Other

17. Why?_____
_____

18. Check the box if you agree with this statement:
☐ I'm confused about these last few questions, and I think I'd like someone who knows more to explain them to me sometime when no one else is around.

19. Had enough questions for one day?

☐ Yes   ☐ No   ☐ Not sure

Thanks for filling this thing out honestly. Really, this can be a GREAT year for you. Let's have a blast!

Application for Admission
Sunday Nite!

For Office Use
Date received _____

NAME _____ PHONE (_____) _____
          Last   First   Middle   Area
                              (Underline the name you go by)

ADDRESS _____
          Number and Street   City   State/Province   Zip/Zone

Birth Date ____/____/____ Sex ____ SSN _____-____-_____ U.S. Citizen? ____ Other _____
                                                                                                                              Country

ARE YOU MARRIED? ____Yes ____No   Name of Spouse:_____

NAME OF PARENT(S) / GUARDIAN(S) _____

_____
          (address if different than above)   City   State/Province   Zip/Zone

School _____
                              Name of School   Graduation Date

_____
          City

START / **FINISH**

Please draw a line connecting the dots | Please find your way through the maze. | Please identify this president by writing his name in the blank

DESIRED ADMISSION STATUS (check one per column)
1 ❏ Weird   2 ❏ Insane   3 ❏ Okay   4 ❏ Great
  ❏ Different   ❏ Obscene   ❏ Normal   ❏ Hero
  ❏ Abnormal

DESIRED DUTIES _____

ACTIVITIES YOU MIGHT PARTICIPATE IN (circle number below)
1. Team Captain   6. Calling   11. Other: _____
2. Egg-sucking   7. Cooking   _____
3. Human sacrifices   8. Spinach-eating
4. Greeting   9. Devoting
5. Artist   10. Leading a prayer group

SPECIAL RECOGNITION (honors, awards, letters, war injuries, etc.) _____

_____

CHURCH _____
                              Name   City   State/Province
Denomination _____ Pastor _____

(Please complete the question on the reverse side and sign.)

1. How did you first learn of Sunday Nite?

2. What influenced you to apply?

3. If you have been out of it for a period of time, please describe what you have been doing.

4. Tell us about yourself. (interests, goals, education, hobbies, and other experiences that have contributed to making you the person you are today)

_____   _____
Signature   Date

When your application has been completed, take one of the following steps:
1. Turn and lick the ar-pit of the person sitting next to you.
2. Bite youuur cat's tail. If you have no cat, or he has no tail, bite your best friend.
3. Return this silly application to a sponsor, roll your eyes, and say, "That was stupid."

19

3. A picture should be included if at all possible. Have a picture day and snap a shot of every kid in the group. Any picture will do, however.

4. Medications, hobbies, interests, boyfriend or girlfriend, car, problems, talents, peculiarities.

5. On the back, an up-to-date progress report can be kept. When the student makes a significant comment, makes a decision for Christ, participates in a special way, include it on the card.

It is important that this file be kept as up-to-date as possible. It will enable you to be more effective in dealing with your kids on a personal, thoughtful, and responsible level.

```
Name _____
Address _____
City _____ State _____ Zip code _____
Phone _____ Email _____
School _____ Grade _____ Age _____
Parents _____
Siblings _____
Interests _____
Friends _____          photo here
Other information _____
_____
_____
_____
```

•Youth Group Registration Card.

One of the most effective ways to build the image of a youth group and create an identity of its own is by using a registration card similar to the example shown below. At each weekly meeting (preferably an outreach meeting) cards are passed out to every kid as they come in the door, whether they are new kids or old-timers. When everyone fills out a card, visitors don't feel like they are being trapped or pressured. At the close of the meeting, all the cards are passed in at the door by dropping them in a box.

A good registration card should avoid looking "churchy," or of the kind used in the regular church services. Also church terminology (membership, baptism, salvation, etc.) should be avoided. An ideal registration card should include the following:

1. A place for your group's trademark or logo.

2. A blank space that can be used for anything. Each week you can use it for something different. For example, have kids draw a picture of the pastor on it, or kids can write messages to you in it, or have a contest in which kids write in the answer to how many beans are in a jar, etc. This keeps the card from getting old, and kids will look forward to it.

3. A place for kids to express a desire, such as being put on the regular mailing list, wanting to become a member, wanting an appointment with you, etc. The wording should be casual and to the point.

```
   REGISTRATION
      * CARD *

   ┌─────────────────────┐
   │    "BLANK SPACE"    │
   │                     │
   │                     │
   └─────────────────────┘

   ☐ SEND ME YOUR REGULAR ANNOUNCE-
   MENTS CONCERNING YOUR GROUP.

   ☐ I AM INTERESTED IN BECOMING A
   REGULAR PART OF YOUR GROUP.

   ☐ I WOULD LIKE SOME SUGGESTIONS
   AND HELPS TO KNOW MORE ABOUT GOD
   AND THE CHRISTIAN LIFE.

   NAME _____
   ADDRESS _____
   CITY _____ ZIP _____
   SCHOOL _____
   PHONE _____ GRADE _____
```

4. The usual name, address, and the like. Add "If this is your first time, fill out below" under the name line, to save the old-timers some work, if you like.

POSTER REGISTRATION

Keeping track of who was present at a major event can be difficult with a larger youth group. Here's a solution. Make a special poster and attach a pen on a string to it; then encourage everyone to write his or her name on it. Ask visitors to write the name of the person they came with as well as their own name. This will give you the opportunity to contact them later. After the event is over, the poster can be used to decorate the youth group meeting room. *David Rasmussen*

COMPUTER PHOTOS

Photographs can easily be put on computer disk to be put in newsletters, on prayer cards for your church family, or in your own youth directory. The most cost-efficient means of doing this is to schedule a day to photograph everyone in the youth group. The film can be processed and put on disk at the same time. Students who can't be there to be photographed can provide photos that can be shipped and processed on a separate disk. Ordering information for photos on disk is available from Seattle Film Works, 1-800-FILMWORKS or http://www.filmworks.com/.

SPECIAL EVENT CHECKLIST

A special event checklist (see page 22) should save you lots of headaches when you plan your next special event. It will minimize little surprises when its time for the event—like someone forgot the refreshments, the tickets weren't ready on time, no one was assigned to bring the change, etc. *Larry Prahl*

VIDEO ASSOCIATION

Just moved to a large group and having a difficult time remembering the names of your kids? Take paper, felt-tip pens, tape, and a camcorder with you to the next youth meeting. During refreshment time, arrange for each student to write his or her name and school on a sheet of paper and tape it to his or her shirt front. Then circulate among the students with the camcorder. Any time you want to refresh your memory and reconnect names and faces, pop in the video. Plus it makes for an amusing time at a party a year later. *Jerry Meadows*

YEARLY PLANNING SURVEY

Surveys can often be very helpful in determining a group's needs and in evaluating your own ministry. The survey on pages 23-24 gets at four different areas: doctrinal understanding (questions 1-9), self-concept (questions 10-19), the youth group (questions 20-30), and personal spiritual growth (questions 31-39). Let the kids know that you don't want their names—just their honest answers.

Give this survey to your group at the beginning of the year and you can refer to it throughout the year in your planning. Give it to them again at the beginning of the next year to see where your group has improved and where you need to place more emphasis. *Ben Sharpton*

WEEKLY PLANNING SHEET

If you have trouble getting organized each week for your youth group meetings and activities, create a weekly planning sheet (see the sample). It will help you to think through what needs to be

---

Youth Group Planning Sheet

Title of event/meeting: _____
Date: _____ Time allocation: _____
Goals: _____
_____
Meal prepared by: _____
Phone no.: _____
Announcements: _____
_____
Activity: _____
    1. Materials needed: _____
    2. Cost: _____
    3. Transportation by: _____
        Phone No.: _____
Songs: _____
Scripture to study: _____
Title: _____
Purpose: _____
Further expressions of worship: _____
Lesson outline: _____
Alternate backup activity: _____
    1. Materials needed: _____
    2. Cost: _____
To do next week: _____
Visit or phone these people: _____
_____
_____
Prayer items: _____
_____Kids' reactions/responses to the
meeting: _____
Future ideas: _____

Evening Rating

1 2 3 4 5 6 7 8 9 10
Pitiful   Excellent

---

done. Set it up on your personal computer if possible. Give detailed copies to your youth advisors, pastor, youth council, and others. Create your own sheet to fit the needs of your program. *Bill Hughes*

SPECIAL EVENT CHECKLIST

What's happening? _____

_____

_____

Date? _____

Time or Schedule? _____

Alternative date? _____

Where? _____

_____

Special preparations? _____

_____

Special equipment?

_____

Who is it happening for? _____

Estimated attendance? _____

Can kids bring friends? _____

The charge? _____ per _____

To whom? _____

Where does any profit go? _____

Registration slip or parental permission slip?

_____

Who will prepare it? _____

_____

Is there a limited number who may register?
_____ If yes, how many? _____

Who is responsible for contacting those invited?

_____

_____

Media? _____

By what date? _____

(P) Phone (L) Letter (PC) Postcard (W) Worship
bulletin (E) Email (O) Other,

specify _____

By what date must slips and/or money be
returned? _____

Return to whom? _____

Make check payable to: _____

Emergency numbers? _____

To be published? _____

Is there a money break for early registration?
_____ By what date? _____

How much? _____ Refunds? _____

Any specific rules or regulations? _____

What? _____

Transportation plans needed? _____

_____

Cost? _____ Who pays? _____

Organizer? _____

Accommodations necessary? _____

Cost? _____ Who pays? _____

Organizer? _____

Meals or food necessary? _____

_____

Cost? _____ Who pays? _____

Organizer? _____

Special purchases necessary? _____

_____

Who will get? _____ By what date? ____

Special equipment participants must bring? ___

_____

_____

Cleanup? _____ Who is responsible? _____

_____

Should participants be notified to bring extra
money? _____ Amount? _____

Spiritual aspects? _____

_____

_____

Who is responsible? _____

Extra adult chaperons necessary? _____

If so, how many? _____

Who will get them? _____

By what date? _____

Do any adult officials have to be notified? ____

If yes, who? _____

Position? _____

_____

Who will notify? _____

By what date? _____

Must any special forms be filled out? _____

If yes, which forms? _____

_____

Who will fill out? _____

By what date? _____

Yearly Planning Survey

	This is me	Not sure	This isn't me
1. I have accepted Jesus as my personal savior.			
2. I believe that the only way for a person to be happy is to know Christ.			
3. I believe that prayers are answered.			
4. I believe that it is important for Christians to witness for Christ.			
5. I know what my spiritual gifts are.			
6. I believe that the Bible is the true Word of God.			
7. I often doubt that God really exists.			
8. I believe that Jesus was a great man, but that's about it.			
9. I believe in life after death including a literal heaven and hell.			
10. On the whole, I am satisfied with myself.			
11. I have some bad habits I'd like to get rid of.			
12. I tend to be a lonely person.			
13. People come to me for advice.			
14. I am considered popular by most people.			
15. I wish I had more respect for myself.			
16. I make good grades in school.			
17. I like to watch and participate in sports.			
18. I feel no one knows the real me.			
19. My family is very important to me.			
20. My church youth group is a high priority in my life.			
21. Youth group meets many of my needs.			
22. Some of the other members of the youth group are my closest friends.			
23. I think this group is too clique orientated.			
24. I often feel left out of the youth group.			
25. I think youth group needs a lot of improvement.			
26. I would like to have more fun and recreation at youth group meetings.			
27. I attend youth group primarily because my folks make me.			
28. I'd like to bring my friends to youth group.			
29. Our youth group has good leaders.			
30. The youth group discussions and activities influence me a great deal.			
31. I have witnessed to at least one person in the last month.			

	This is me	Not sure	This isn't me
32. I am basically very selfish and don't care that much about others.			
33. I enjoy getting together with other Christians.			
34. I enjoy worshipping at church.			
35. I set aside time on a regular basis for personal devotions (Bible reading, prayer, or meditation).			
36. I like to pray with other Christians.			
37. I feel a need to grow deeper in my faith.			
38. I have led someone to Christ before.			
39. I am happy with my involvement in church.			
40. For me, living a Christian life is almost impossible most of the time.			

Strengths of our youth group: _____

_____

Weaknesses of our youth group: _____

_____

_____

Please check five of the following activities that you would like to see our youth group do in the near future:

____beach party

____tubing party

____Halloween party

____movie night

____camping trip

____a dance

____hayride

____go to a ball game

____go to theme park, etc.

____water ski trip

____lock-in

____bowling

____roller skating

____progressive dinner

____bike hike

____trip to different colleges

____weekend retreat

____summer camp

____youth week

____youth-led worship

____put on a play

____have a Christian concert

____go to a concert

____service project of some kind

____have a fundraiser

____have a work camp

____car rally

____other:

_____

RECREATION FILE

A simple file of index cards will help a busy youth worker keep track of people, places, ideas, sources, etc. The following are only a few of the many possible headings for your file:

Agencies—Ministerial	Hiking
Agencies—Social Work	Ideas
Athletics	Indoor Activities
Attendance Boosters	Leadership
Banquets	Development
Camping Equipment	Materials and Curricula
Campsites	Meeting Places
Campus Ministry	Missions and Outreach
Colleges	Multimedia
Conference Centers	Music and Music Groups
Counseling	Outdoor Activities
Counselors—Chaperons	Party Ideas
Creative	Prizes
Communications	Publications
Devotionals	Publicity
Drama	Retreats and Rallies
Films	Service Projects
Fundraising	Speakers
Game Equipment	Special Events
Games	Youth Organizations
Handicrafts	

William L. Chane

ILLUSTRATION FILE

Have you ever found yourself scrounging through old notes, books, and drawers trying to find that great illustration you used a year or so ago? One way to remedy this is to start an illustration file using index cards—or a computer, if you have one.

Whenever you run across a great illustration in a book, article, manual, sermon, tape, or from your own life experience, jot it down and file it away for future use. Next time you have to speak to a group of young people or prepare a lesson, you'll have a wealth of good material to use. *Robert Crosby*

PLANNING SURVEY

Using a survey like the one on page 26 at the beginning of the school year can be very helpful for planning programs and activities. Not only will you get a better idea of what the needs and likes of your students are, but it gives them more of a feeling of participation in the planning of things. Simply print up the surveys, pass them out, and allow the kids to work on them for as long as necessary. After you get the results, you might want to go over them with all the students (and your leaders) to begin implementing the results. *J. Richard Short*

HOW ARE WE DOING?

Wanna hear from those young people and parents who you usually don't hear from? Use the questionnaires on pages 27-28, Make it two-sided: the front for your kids and the back for their parents. Or you can print the survey on two separate sheets if you think your kids or their parents want to keep their answers private from each other. *Craig McClun*

EVENT EVALUATION

Building a consistent youth ministry is a constant yearly challenge. One help for steady improvement is for students to fill out an event evaluation (see page 29). The key to effectiveness is evaluating after each event, recording your data for future planning helps, and using the results when you consider whether to repeat an event or try to develop a new one. The evaluation should be general enough to cover events ranging from a service project to a fellowship banquet to a retreat. *Jim Bourne*

COMPILE YOUR OWN YOUTH MINISTRY BOOK

Create a personalized resource of effective youth ministry ideas you've read about, handouts you've received, or notes you've jotted down during a seminar. Forget traditional stand-up files—instead, edit your own book. Get a three-ring notebook, and every time you read a good article, either photocopy it or cut it out and put it in your notebook. Your evolving handbook may not be on the bestseller list, but you'll have a personalized, practical youth ministry reference work that you can use for a long time. *Bert L. Jones*

Planning Survey

Topics	Methods	Recreation	Service Projects
Circle 10 that most interest you.	Circle 4 that you most enjoy.	Circle 8 that you enjoy.	Circle 6 which you most want to do.

Topics — Circle 10 that most interest you.

1. Alcohol
2. Anger
3. Bible studies
4. Competition
5. Careers
6. Colleges
7. Dating
8. Death
9. Drugs
10. Ecology
11. Faith
12. Getting along with brothers and sisters
13. Getting along with parents
14. Getting along with friends
15. Getting along with adults
16. God's will
17. Group pressure
18. Hunger
19. Identity
20. Independence
21. Jealousy
22. Love
23. Marriage
24. Poverty/Affluence
25. Religion
26. Race
27. Sex
28. School
29. Suburbia
30. Equal rights
31. World Religions
32. Values
Others:
33. _____
34. _____
35. _____

Methods — Circle 4 that you most enjoy.

1. Skits
2. Puppets
3. Making banners
4. Discussion
5. Rapping
6. Panels
7. Movies
8. Music videos
9. Role playing
10. Speakers
11. Group study
12. Workbooks
Others:
13. _____
14. _____
15. _____

Recreation — Circle 8 that you enjoy.

1. Beaches
2. Mountains
3. Skiing
4. Softball
5. Volleyball
6. Over the line
7. Hiking
8. Bicycling
9. Swimming
10. Progressive dinners
11. Pizza parties
12. Horseback riding
13. Miniature golf
14. Tubing
15. Go-karts
16. Bowling
17. Trampolines
18. Roller skating
19. Ice skating
20. Dancing
21. Cookouts
22. Hayrides
23. Square dancing
24. Canoeing
Others:
25. _____
26. _____
27. _____

Service Projects — Circle 6 which you most want to do.

1. Fix up the youth room
2. Christmas caroling
3. Trick-or-Treat for UNICEF
4. Spook house for UNICEF
5. Car wash for world hunger
6. Visit a nursing home
7. Thanksgiving baskets
8. Help at a Salvation Army facility
9. Collect aluminum cans
10. Newspaper drive
11. Visit prospective church members
12. Cook a meal for the congregation to raise money
13. Sponsor a drop-in center for neighborhood youth
14. Adopt an orphan overseas
Others:
15. _____
16. _____
17. _____
18. _____

How Are We Doing?
A Youth Questionnaire

Let us guess—you're busy, but not too busy to have some feelings about our youth group. So here's a convenient way to tell us what you like and don't like. Then mail it to the church. Surveys will be carefully discussed and acted upon.

1. I am in ☐ junior high ☐ senior high

2. How often do you come to youth meetings and events:

   ☐ never   ☐ seldom (twice a year or so)   ☐ occasionally (every other month)

   ☐ usually (twice a month)

3. If you don't attend much, why not? (Write **1** by the most common reason, **2** by the next most common reason, etc.)

   ___Too few games   ___Just not interested

   ___No transportation   ___Friends don't or won't come

   ___I don't like the leaders   ___No time

   ___My job   ___Not challenging enough

   ___Not enough emphasis on the Bible   ___Other: _____

   ___No one's really asked me   _____

4. If you do attend frequently, mark why. (Write 1 by the most common reason, 2 by the next most common reason, etc.)

   ___Food   ___My parents make me come

   ___Study time   ___Not much else to do

   ___Games   ___Leaders are interested in me

   ___Friends who come   ___Other: _____

   ___I like the leaders   _____

   ___Trips and activities   _____

5. Have you invited someone to youth group during ☐ the last week? ☐ the last month? ☐ the last three months?

6. How many adult friends do you have in the church? ☐ several ☐ one or two ☐ none

7. What is the youth group doing now that you like?

8. What should the youth group do differently?

9. What would make you want to attend youth group functions more often?

27

How Are We Doing?
A Parent Questionnaire

Let us guess—you're busy, but not too busy to have some feelings about our youth group. So here's a convenient way to tell us what you like and don't like. Then mail it to the church. Surveys will be carefully discussed and acted upon.

1. How often do you participate in the youth programs? ☐ never ☐ seldom ☐ occasionally ☐ usually

2. What do you like about our youth program? _____
   _____

3. What do you dislike about it? _____
   _____

4. Comment on the youth pastor (0—no opportunity to observe; 1—especially good; 2—okay; 3—needs to improve):

   ___Enjoys being around young people   ___Communicates with young people

   ___Able to get others involved   ___Equally supports young people and their parents

   ___Knows the Bible   ___Has leadership abilities

   ___Applies the Bible in practical ways to kids' lives   ___Recruits youth workers

   ___Has time for his or her own family   ___Counsels young people

   ___Provides helping resources for young people and their families   ___Has organizational skills

   ___Listens to young people (their opinions, problems, etc.)   ___Plans ahead

   ___Delegates work   ___Know how to manage his or her time

5. What specific suggestions do you have for your youth pastor? (Include specific suggestions for improving areas listed in question 4 above.) _____

6. What comments or suggestions do you have for the youth leaders? _____
   _____

7. How can the youth program better help you? _____
   _____
   _____

Event Evaluation

The event I am evaluating is _____

Date of the event _____

I am in _____ grade. ☐ M or ☐ F

Rate the following areas on a scale of one to 10.

1. Build up. Were you aware of the event? How well were you informed? Did you have adequate time to prepare to participate in this event?

|——|——|——|——|
1   2   3   4   5
Definitely no!   Definitely yes!

2. Objectives. Did you understand the goals of the event and do you think those goals were met?

|——|——|——|——|
1   2   3   4   5
Definitely no!   Definitely yes!

3. Value. Was the event valuable? Was it worth participating in? Was it something you thought was important for youths to consider?

4. Interest. Did it meet a need or interest that you have? Did it benefit you in your Christian growth? Was it helpful for Christian living?

|——|——|——|——|
1   2   3   4   5
Definitely no!   Definitely yes!

5. Leadership. Did the leaders seem prepared? Did they present the material thoroughly? Did you feel they tried to do a good job?

|——|——|——|——|
1   2   3   4   5
Definitely no!   Definitely yes!

6. Repeatability. Would you recommend repeating this event? Do you think an annual event of this type would be good?

|——|——|——|——|
1   2   3   4   5
Definitely no!   Definitely yes!

7. What did you especially like? _____

_____

8. What needed to be improved? _____

_____

DEMOGRAPHICS MAP

Whether yours is an urban, suburban, or rural church, your youth group members may be spread out all over the county—or wider. If you need a visual handle on the location of your teenagers (for purposes of planning socials, transportation, car pools, prayer groups, etc.), use a large, detailed street map (available from your local department of transportation among other places). Use numbered pushpins to identify the location of each church family with teenagers; include a key that matches numbers with family names. *Tom Lytle*

CLIP ART FILE

Have all youth leaders keep an eye out for unique, unusual, or just plain strange graphics, art, and photos in newspaper and magazines. Cut them out and place them in a central file that is available when you create flyers or mailers for your group. Look also for unusual type or catch phrases. Cut and paste parts of them together to create sharp graphics. You can ask the whole group to look for good stuff. Keep a box in your office or in the group meeting room for any contributions. *James Taylor*

PROGRAMMING HINTS

MEET AT THE SPOT

Have you ever had the problem of your young people not knowing where to meet for different activities and social events? Have you ever had young people come to the church and leave, simply because they did not know where to meet? Here is a solution. Find a convenient place in your church parking lot. Here, paint on the pavement a large circle, about five or six feet in diameter. Use brightly colored epoxy paint. Then call this place The Spot.

Very soon your young people will know exactly where to meet when you say, "Meet at the Spot." Not only is this idea practical, but it's also novel. The Spot will have a personality all its own. *Andrew Pryor*

SIGNS OF GOOD TIMES

Here's a way to make those mountaintop experiences last a little longer. Next time you take your kids to a camp, retreat, conference, or elsewhere they have a memorable experience, make or have made a sign for the event that's on display throughout the event. It can be made of anything—cloth, wood, plastic, poster board—as long as it's fairly durable. The sign can have the name of the event, the name of the group, the theme of the event, a Bible verse, the date—anything you feel is meaningful.

When the event is over, take the sign down and have all the kids who attended sign their names on it with a permanent marker. If there's room, they can also write a thought. The sign can then be brought back to your youth group meeting room and displayed as a reminder of the event. *David P. Mahoney*

INCREDIBLE PRIZES!

Have you ever wanted to give away some truly exciting prizes for games and giveaways, but couldn't because of the expense? Then this idea is for you!

Go through magazines or catalogs and cut out pictures of some incredible prizes—a new car, a complete stereo system, a trip to Hawaii. You might also cut out a few less-than-incredible prizes as

well—a pair of socks, a can of motor oil, a tube of toothpaste. Seal them in envelopes.

Play your games or have your contests; and when it's time for the awarding of prizes, have the winners pick an envelope. They can't tell what's in it, but it could be a picture of an incredible prize. When the prize is revealed, you can make a big deal out of it—with all the typical fanfare, announce, "CONGRATULATIONS! YOU'VE JUST WON A PICTURE OF A BRAND-NEW FULLY-EQUIPPED WINNEBAGO MOTOR HOME!" or "YOU'VE JUST WON A PICTURE OF TWO POUNDS OF DOG BISCUITS!"

Even though no one is really winning anything, the kids will really get into the competition of seeing who can win the most valuable picture, and all it costs the youth group is a few envelopes and some old catalogs. *Gene Defries*

LET'S TALK

Put some variety into your youth group programming with a different approach to your meetings for each week of the month. Here's an example:
• Week One. "Let's Hear"—Feature a guest speaker or other special presentation.
• Week Two. "Let's Talk"—A discussion or study with lots of good dialogue and discussion.
• Week Three. "Let's Do"—An action-oriented meeting that involves the teenagers in activities, planning, service, etc.
• Week Four. "Let's Go"—A field trip or media presentation exposing the group to a new situation or environment.
• Week Five (when there is one). "Let's Eat"—Have a potluck, pizza bash, or other gastronomical event. Kids will look forward to those months with a fifth week! *Joe Weatherly*

HEEEEERE'S JOHNNY!

Youth meetings can start getting a little less-than-exciting if they are done in the same format all the time. One way to change things a little is to set up your youth group meeting like a talk show. This is especially good if you have special guests.

Set up the front of the room with a couch for the guests and a desk and chair for the host. The kids can be the studio audience, listening as well as asking questions of the guest. You might even want to have someone videotape the whole thing for "broadcast in a later time zone." *Roger J. Rome*

PICTORIAL RETREAT REPORT

After the next retreat or camp, don't just send two or three kids up to the pulpit during the evening service to highlight the weekend for the congregation—show a video. Lay out a scrapbook of the weekend in the lobby too.

Of course, this requires that someone take a smooth video. And encouraging kids to bring their cameras and take snapshots for the scrapbook provides the congregation with each student's unique perspective of the event. *Dale Shackley*

POSTCARD HOME

After a retreat or a lesson that causes your kids to commit to something or change in some way, hand each student a prestamped post card (or a 4x6 index card—the post office won't take 3x5 cards). Ask your students to write to themselves what they feel God leading them to do or change—you won't need to tell them what to write. Then ask them to write their address on the other side. The next day you drop the cards in the mail. A perfect auto-reminder! *Gerard Labrecque*

PHONE DEVOTIONAL

Here's a good way to help kids with their devotions, and to do some creative outreach ministry as well. Set up a daily youth devotional phone line with its own private number. The phone company can arrange one for you at reasonable rates. Give the phone number a clever name, like "T.N.T. (Totally Necessary Telephone) LINE" or whatever. The phone company might help you find a number that is easy for kids to remember. You will also need a telephone answering device.

The idea is for kids to call the number every day for a short devotional message. This means, of course, that you (or someone else) will have to change the message every day. It can include a short passage of Scripture and a thought for the day. If you wish you can also include some information about the youth group.

To use this idea for outreach, have your youth group members distribute attractive business cards that display the phone number and a phrase like "Call for a dynamite life every day." Many "outside" kids who might not come to church or the youth group will call and be exposed to the Gospel. On weekends you might change the theme and have one or two of your kids share their testimonies on the tape. Kids love to use the phone, so here's a good way to take advantage of it! *Steve French*

INVITE A DRAMA GROUP

Most high school drama classes put on a play or two during the course of the school year. Usually these drama students work for months rehearsing their lines, creating costumes and building sets. Then they put the play on for the student body or their parents, and it's all over.

Most drama classes would welcome the chance to find another audience for a production in which

they've invested so much time. Find out what plays your high school drama group plans to put on this year, and if the play sounds acceptable for a Christian youth group meeting, invite the group to present their production to your group. They could even use the youth group for a dress rehearsal.

Often you can use the play as the basis for a talk or devotional (many plays deal with values), and it will serve as a great introduction to the youth group for many of the drama kids. *David C. Wright*

INVISIBLE INK GROUPS

Here's an easy way to move kids into groups or teams. When they arrive, mark on their hands or their necks with invisible fluorescent ink (like the type used at amusement parks to stamp your hand for reentry). Don't tell them what it says. You can use a rubber stamp to apply the marks, or you can put them on with a pen or brush. The ink is available in stationery, art, or novelty shops.

When it's time for the kids to get into groups, turn off the lights and have them get under a black light to see which group they're in. You can use codes, like an O for group one and X for group two, and so on. Kids enjoy the mystery that's involved and it's an effective way to get them into groups without lots of arguing and changing from one group to the next. *Mitch Olson*

FREE FAST FOOD

Running out of ways to reward kids for fundraisers and contests? Try fast-food coupons, which many restaurant chains gladly give you or sell you at a discount. Wait for a slow time during the day, then go in, ask for the manager, tell the manager who you are and what you do. Good responses are reported from McDonald's, Taco Bell, Dairy Queen, Long John Silver's, Noble Roman's Pizza, and others (at least in some parts of the country). Your kids will love fast-food coupons—and they won't break your youth budget. *Dale Shackley*

CARD GROUPS

Use a deck of common playing cards to randomly divide a larger group into smaller groups. First sort the deck into suits (hearts, spades, diamonds, clubs), using as many suits as you want to have groups. Then arrange each suit in ascending order (from 2 to ace) and place in a separate stack. Now create one stack by taking the top card from each stack, then the next card from each (in the same order), and so on through the deck.

As kids enter the meeting place, hand each one a card from the top of the deck and ask them to hold on to them until time to divide up into groups. To form groups, have all the people with the same suit come together. *John Larson*

ROTATING SUNDAY SCHOOL

Liven up Sunday school for junior high kids with short attention spans by keeping them on the move.

Brainstorm possible content and illustrations for an upcoming Sunday school lesson with your staff of teachers. Ask each teacher to take one of the ideas the group comes up with and prepare a mini-lesson for the designated Sunday. Length? Probably five to 10 minutes, depending on how many mini-lessons you'll offer and how long your entire class time lasts. You may want to allow time for a closing all-group session.

As students arrive that Sunday, randomly assign them to where teachers are waiting. Signal the end of each mini-lesson with a gong or other jarring instrument. Signal the end of the first lesson and explain to the kids how to find their next class—for example, rotate clockwise to the next teacher or room. By the end of Sunday school, all the junior highers should have met with all the teachers. *Jeff Elliott*

DISTINCTIVE DATES

The following dates, taken from Chases' Calendar of Annual Events (Apple Tree Press, Flint, Michigan), can be used in several different ways. Combined with some imagination they can be used as party or special program themes, attention-getters in letters, etc.

- **January** (Louisiana Yam Supper Season)
  - 2-8   Save-the-Pun Week (have a pun party)
  - 7   Bulfinch Exchange Festival in Fukuoka, Japan
- **February**
  - 4-6   Iceworm Festival in Cordova, Alaska
  - 6-9   Annual Camel-Wrestling Competition in Yenipazar, Turkey
  - 7-11   National Pay-Your-Bills Week
- **March** (International Hamburger-Pickle Month)
  - 1-5   Return-Your-Borrowed-Book Week
  - 6-11   National Procrastination Week
  - 15   Buzzard Day in Hinkley, Ohio
- **April** (Anti-Noise Month)
  - 3-9   National Laugh Week
  - 1-9   Daffodil Festival in Puyallup, Washington
  - 6-15   National Artichoke Week
  - 22-26   National Baby Week
- **May** (Car-Care Month, International Play-Your-Own-Harpsichord Month, Senior Citizens Month)
  - 18-27   International Pickle Week (see March)
- **June** (Cat-and-Kitten Month, Fight-the-Filthy-Fly Month, National Ragweed-Control Month)
  - 4-10   Girl-Watching Week
  - 15   Dragon Boat Festival in Hong Kong
  - 17-18   Fudge-Off Finals in Mackinac Island, Michigan (dedicated to improving the art of making fudge)
  - 17   National Hollering Contest in Dunn, North Carolina
  - 19-25   National Fink Week (aimed at restoring dignity "to the honorable surname of Fink")

- 24   National Rooster-Crowing Contest in Grants Pass, Oregon
- **July** (National Hot Dog Month, National Barbecue Month, Souvenir Month)
  - 2   Stone Skipping and Ge-Plunking Open Tournament on Mackinac Island
  - 7-9   Custer's Last Stand Reenactment in Hardin, Montana (from the Indian point of view)
- **August** (Sandwich Month)
  - 1-6   National Clown Week
  - 4   Lizzie Borden Liberation Day
  - 11-12   Hobo Convention in Britt, Iowa

- 19   National Chimneys Jousting Tournament in Mt. Solon, Virginia
- 24   National Hula-Hoop Championships in Hollywood
- **September** (American Youth Month)
  - 2   Mustache Day
  - 6   Be-Late-for-Something Day, sponsored by the Procrastinator's Club of America
  - 24-30   National Dog Week
- **October** (Country Music Month, Gourmet Adventures Month, Pizza Festival Month)
  - 2-8   Newspaper Week
  - 5-14   National Macaroni Week
  - 9-15   International Letter-Writing Week
  - 25-Nov.2   National Pretzel Week
  - 29-Nov.4   National Mushroom Week
- **November** (Think-of-What-You-Can-Replace-With-Plastic Month)
  - 5-11   International Cat Week
  - 13-17   National Split-Pea-Soup Week
  - 21-27   Elderly Gentlemen Week
  - 23-Jan.1   National Indigestion Season (proclaimed by the baking soda people)

- **December** (Model Railroad Month)
  - 2   Whirling Dervish Festival in Konya, Turkey
  - 16   Man-Will-Never-Fly Memorial Day (celebrated by the Man-Will-Never-Fly Society)
  - 21   Forefather's Day (commemorating the Pilgrim's landing)
  - 31   Day of the Namahage in Japan (sluggards are given an opportunity to change their minds and go to work or be punished by devils)

Dan Fields

SHORT STORIES AND SCRIPTURE

The modern short story can be a creative and effective tool for communicating scriptural truths. Oscar Wilde's "Happy Prince," for example, can be used to introduce social concerns to youth; Nathaniel Hawthorne's "Young Goodman Brown" may spark a lively discussion of the human condition.

Most public and university libraries subscribe to The Short Story Index, a periodically updated, topical index to short stories in anthologies. If you're interested on a short piece on peace making, for example, you check each volume of the Index under peace, nonviolence, pacifism, and related topics, noting the short stories listed there and the anthologies in which they appear. Then check the library database to locate the anthologies and review them to find the most promising story for your purposes.

Needless to say, each story should be evaluated for its appropriateness as reading material for Christian youth. Though many of the pieces indexed will not present biblical viewpoints, they can serve as starting points for discussing what a biblical perspective would be. *Steve Perisho*

QUESTION BOX

Construct a box with a slit in the top that can be used to receive questions that the kids in your group would like answered. Place the box in a conspicuous place in the meeting room and allow kids to drop their questions (on any subject) into the box each week. Allow time each week during the meeting to answer questions that were submitted the week before. This is a very good way to keep your finger on the pulse of the group. *Karen Shager*

PROMOTION

YOUTH GROUP HOTLINE

Here is a good way to keep your teens informed about coming events and to give them a way to leave messages for you. If you don't have a private office or phone line available to you at church, purchase an extra phone line for your home and put a for-teens-only message on your answering machine (maybe your church will pay for it). Change the message every day. Provide news of coming events, a thought for the day, jokes, or whatever. Invite kids to leave messages for you. You will find that both the young people and their parents will use such a hotline. The charge for the extra line is usually small enough to make it easily affordable. *Steve Swanson*

YOUTH GROUP DOLLARS

Here's a good way to increase attendance at your youth group activities and meetings. Award play money at each event that can be redeemed at a later date for discounts on camp, special outings, prizes that kids can bid on, or whatever. Kids get one every time they attend a group function. Kids should initial them immediately.

Or create your own play money—Baptist bucks, Covenant currency, youth group gold. Create them on your personal computer or on paper and make lots of copies on colorful paper. *Molly Halter*

SUMMER CALENDAR CASSETTE

With the proliferation of low-cost audio duplicating equipment, why not create something less expensive than a summer calendar this year—like a summer calendar cassette?

Write out in script form all the information you'd put on a normal calendar; choose some hot Christian music that fits the different events; and recruit someone with good pipes (that's broadcast lingo for a good radio voice), with some broadcasting experience, and with access to a recording studio. Use the music to open and close the audio calendar, for background, or for bridges between announcements. (Be sure to secure permission on copyrighted music.)

Now duplicate your master tape on inexpensive cassette blanks, design a fun cover letter, and mail them to your teenagers. Your cassette calendar may become a summer tradition! *Dave Mahoney*

Balloon Signs

Next time you need to hang a sign in a large room where everyone can see it, try this: Fill a few balloons with helium and tie the sign to them. The balloons will go to the ceiling and take the sign with them.

This works especially well at camps and conferences where you need to register hundreds of kids. Normally each table has a sign to indicate which person should go to it, according to the initials of their last names. Put those signs in the air with balloons—and the signs will be easily spotted.

This technique can also be used for large group games when you need to mark various locations, boundaries, etc., in the room. Works great! *David Washburn*

G.Y.M. at Church

Sometimes the success of a group has a lot to do with its name. Here's an idea for one. Call your youth group G.Y.M., which stands for great youth meeting. Then capitalize on the acronym in your events and organization. Your meeting place can now be called the GYM-nasium, your youth sponsors can be called coaches, your activities can be called work-outs, and your weekly newsletter can be entitled "Gym Shorts." You can carry out the theme as far as you wish. It's an idea that's no sweat. *Jim Mitchell*

Super Summer Sign-Up Center

Do you spend too many summer Sundays registering kids and taking money for camps, amusement-park trips, concerts?

Try this instead. Make a stand four feet tall or so (see diagram). Attach pockets to the stand to hold summer calendars, flyers, brochures, general announcements, and photos from the previous summer's events. Then attach wild letters that say SUPER SUMMER SIGN-UP CENTER to the stand.

Encourage the teens and their parents to consult the center every Sunday and to register there for various events. Recruit kids or sponsors to man

the center before, between, and after services. Be sure to stock the center with envelopes, pencils, forms, and a locking cash box.

Make registration even more painless by printing a Super Summer Sign-Up Certificate—a sheet that lists all the summer's activities, dates, and costs. All kids have to do is mark the events they want to attend, total what they're paying for those events, place both the certificate and a check or cash in an envelope, and turn it in to the sign-up center. You can mail the certificates to your group in May so they can plan at home and bring the form already completed to your meeting. *Dave Mahoney*

Poster of the Month

This idea can increase attendance and provide kids with some wholesome decorations for their bedrooms.

Each month purchase an attractive poster with a message (most Christian bookstores carry them), and on the first Sunday of the month post it in the youth group meeting place. If you can't find suitable posters, make your own—go to any bookstore or Hallmark shop or record shop and buy a secular poster and add a Christian message or Bible verse.

On the fourth Sunday of each month, offer the poster as a door prize. Kids will enjoy taking them home and putting them up in their rooms. *David Washburn*

JIGSAW MIXER

If your group is like most, you'll usually have a few kids who always come early to your meetings. Often they sit around and act bored, or they run off somewhere and wind up being late when the meeting actually starts.

To remedy this, provide a big jigsaw puzzle on a table in the back of the room which can be worked on by anyone who comes early. A 400- to 600-piece puzzle should keep kids busy for weeks. When the puzzle is finished, make it into a poster using puzzle glue, and hang it in the room or give it to someone. This activity is creative, group-building, thought-provoking, and decorative! *Keith Curran*

NAME-TAG HATS

When two or more youth groups combine for a special function, name tags are helpful—but boring. A different approach is to make name-tag hats. You

can make them yourself, or get them from a variety of fast-food places that make them for children. Long John Silver's, for example, has a pirate hat that can be turned inside out, leaving plenty of white space to write or decorate for a name-tag hat. Most fast-food places welcome the free publicity and will give you all you need.

Name-tag hats are not only fun to wear, but can improve eye contact. People look up rather than down. *Bruce Johnson*

HOW TO MAKE A YOUTH PASTOR'S DAY

Looking for a way to convey to your kids in a tactful way how frustrating they can be to you? Without being heavy-handed or whiny, can you tell them how they make your job more difficult than it needs to be?

Adapt for your group "A Special Message from Your Leader"—a leaflet that whimsically addresses your gripes and good-naturedly suggests alternatives. It is ideal for publication in a youth group newsletter. *Jack White*

How to Make Jack's Day

A top youth group member—

• Tells Jack he looks like Brad Pitt/Michael Jordan/Jim Carey.

• Doesn't leave Big Mac containers and french fries in someone's car when she gets dropped off.

• Doesn't leave his copy of the Bible study take-home notes on someone's sofa when he goes home. (Ask Derrick how to treat Bible study notes...)

• Comes to events with a smile on her face.

• Looks for ways he can help others.

• Knows what's going on in the youth group—and if she can't remember, she calls the Not-So-Hot Line (429-8915).

• Loves retreats, tells his friends about them, saves for them, and can't wait for the next one!

• Is not rich, but still pays her way, pays on time, and occasionally offers to pay for someone who is new, short of cash, or undecided about going.

• Asks the leaders if there is any responsibility he can take to make things easier on the leaders and to gain experience in the process.

• Uses a generous amount of deodorant —especially on Camp Lewis retreats.

• Is willing to compromise for the good of the youth group when it comes to finding a place to eat, selecting activities, etc.

• Doesn't complain about activities, realizing the awesome effort the leaders made. Instead, the TYGM offers suggestions for the future—and when an activity bombs, she's tactful about it.

- Refrains from suggesting that we go to Meadowlands Race Track.
- Tells the leader (sooner than the last minute) what time he has to be home.
- Invites new people to special events and activities.
- Brings her Bible to Bible studies.
- Does not say "I'm coming" when he actually has no intention of showing up.
- Offers the last slice of pizza to the leader.
- Invites her friends to her youth group instead of letting them talk her into going to a weekend party.
- Comes to Jell-O Nite even though she doesn't like Jell-O.
- Is willing to forget the activities that bomb and instead reflects on the ones that succeed.
- Sends a thank-you note to Jack or other leaders when the occasion calls for it.
- Supplies refreshments unexpectedly once in a blue moon.
- Doesn't expect to get all the time, but considers giving, too.
- Sets a good example for the younger kids, and tells them how excited she is they'll be in the youth group one day.
- Knows how to have a good time without getting out of hand.
- Doesn't criticize others to make himself look good.
- Does her best to straighten up the room, cabin, bus, etc., before leaving.
- Does not sneeze on his neighbor's McNuggets.
- Opens doors for the young women in the group.
- Shows respect to her parents, whether or not they are believers.
- Desires to be involved in the life of the local church.
- Drives responsibly whenever he drives for the youth group.
- Doesn't try to sneak out of a commitment.
- Is willing to come to February's work projects as well as to August's Super-Duper Saturday All-Day Ski Party.
- Is above fabricating stories to avoid attending a youth group function she's not crazy about.
- Treats his date kindly and respectfully.
- Doesn't blab to all her girlfriends what she doesn't like about Moose.
- Welcomes new members, realizing they're probably nervous and unsure of themselves.
- Doesn't hog the ping-pong table, doesn't drink all the pineapple soda, and doesn't yak so much that no one else can get a word in edgewise.

YOUTH LEADER'S COUPON BOOK

If you can't afford to give a Christmas or birthday present to every young person in your group, try this. It's an inexpensive but valuable gift idea.

★ Good for one free dinner at my house.
★ Good for one free private conversation (void between midnight and 6:00 a.m.
★ Good for prayer for any prayer request.
★ Good for one free ride (in an emergency) to the destination of your choice (within reason).
★ Good for one encouraging word. Redeemable any time. H Good for one free pat on the back when needed.
★ Good for one pretty good answer to your most burning question.
★ Good for one evening of baby-sitting. We have the baby, you do the sitting (for free, of course).
★ Good for one treasure map: A free treasure will be given to anyone who visits the youth pastor's office Monday through Friday between 9:00 a.m. and 4:30 p.m. Call for an appointment.

Create a coupon book that offers a variety of services to kids, redeemable any time during the year. Think up as many coupons as you like. These coupons offer kids something for free and makes them aware of your concern for them. *Larry J. Stoffel*

GLOVE BOX STICKERS

Like most youth workers, you're probably a part-time chauffeur, too. Because your students spend a lot of time in your car, try putting a catchy bumper

sticker or an especially funny or appropriate comic strip on your dashboard or glove box. They can be convenient conversation starters for you, especially if it's a student's first time riding home with you. Plus it also gives teenagers a good excuse to start conversations about tough or touchy subjects. *Julie Bowe*

A FRIEND FOR ALL TIME

The poem on page 39 was written by a youth worker for one of his young people. You might find it to be useful at a senior banquet or a year-end party. It could be read, accompanied by music or a video, or use it as an inscription in books and Bibles. *Dan Engle*

GENERIC GREETING CARDS

It's always a good idea to remember your young people by sending them birthday cards, get well cards, thank you cards, and the like. But keeping an inventory of all those cards can strain your storage space, right?

So create your own generic card. You will be able to change it easily if you create it on your personal computer, but it's okay just to lay it out on paper. Be sure to write a personal note on each card. *Alan C. Wilder*

Here's how to make it:

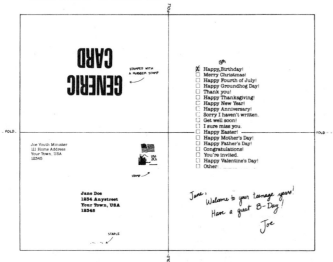

GETTING TO KNOW YOU

Just arrived in your new youth-working position? Wondering how to get to know all those kids? Insert your name in the following offer, and include it in your next church newsletter or bulletin. You'll get lots of takers. *Dan Lambert*

Chores with Dan

I'd like to get to know all of you high schoolers here at Community Church better, so here's a plan to do just that (which I'll probably regret).

Remember that chore you simply hate or always wish you had help with? List below the date and time this month you have to do that chore—and I'll come help you. I figure that this way, I'll not only get to know you, but I'll better understand the things you do. (Not to mention the great stories you can tell about what you made me do.)
YES! I want Dan to help me,
_____, on _____.
He needs to be at my house at _____.
My address is _____.
He should bring an extra set of clothes: ☐ Yes ☐ No
Special instructions:_____
_____.

PRAYER LETTER

One good way to care for your young people is to pray for them individually. If you do this you might want to let them know with a personal letter similar to the one below. Each day, choose one or two teens for prayer and a special note. Here's a sample:

Dear Becca,
Hi! Hope you are having a great year in school! You know, you are special to me and our church. I don't tell you that enough, but I want you to know it. This morning you were the subject of my quiet time. I prayed that God would be especially close to you today and help you with your everyday problems and victories. God truly loves you and wants only the best for you. I do, too.

In Christ,
Jim

James Bourne

A Friend for All Time

There is no knowing how God puts it in the minds of certain people,
to be in a certain place, at a certain time—to work, to live, to learn.

Yet, suddenly here we were. At first just faces—just acquaintances,
but with so much in common—so much to share;
a love for God, a zest for life, an interest in others.

In no time at all we were best of friends.
Those once unfamiliar faces turned into the warm smile of a brother.
That one-time acquaintance became the encourager who helped you through exams,
through a heartache, through a problem at home.

We had been full of foreboding, skeptical of being a part of so large a mass of unknowns,
just a drop of water awash in a sea of people. But that place so foreign
soon became home, and we became family.

We are together, we traveled together, we endured awkward and tough times.
And we laughed. And the bond between us grew and grew.
Brothers, sisters, family, friends.

Then, in no time at all, a year had come and gone.
For some there would be a time of parting—graduation, summer jobs, visits with parents,
vacations—there might even be those we wouldn't see for a very long while.

But we knew we had something that would last,
something that years could not take away,
something that would even ripple into forever.
We had a friend for all time.

FACILITIES

CREATIVE CARPETING

If your youth budget is limited and your youth room looks like a dungeon, spend some time with your kids obtaining carpet fragments or samples. Then have the entire youth group, with glue and sewing needles, carpet their youth room. Not only do the kids have fun, but they will feel like the place is their room. *John Coulombe*

GRAFFITI RULES!

If you have a meeting room which is used exclusively by your youth group, give the kids one or two walls to graffiti with anything they want. Provide paint, spray paint, and brushes, and let the kids be creative. You might want to make one rule about public decency; but otherwise, let the kids say what they want. You can always paint over it later and try again. *Steve Gladen*

MAILBOXES

In the days of the glass soda bottle you could find wooden crates for this idea. Today you'll probably have to make your own. Build a mountable wooden box with slots so that each student can have a personal mailbox. Then hang it near your meeting room. It's a convenient way to drop off flyers to your regular teens. It also helps them communicate with each other, for example, if they have a special note they want to give to someone. All your students will feel important because they have their own little niches. As new people join your group, make sure they receive a mailbox as soon as possible so they feel they belong. *Donna McElrath*

YAK SHAK

One youth group ran a want-ad in the local newspaper, asking for donations of used furniture for the church youth center. Those who gave furniture received receipts for tax purposes and now the group has a big comfortable, casual living room to hold its meetings in. Kids and visitors are much more relaxed in this informal atmosphere and the room has been named the Yak Shak. Try it if your youth meeting room needs redecorating. *Loren Reynolds*

DROP-CLOTH WALL HANGING

Like many church boards, yours will probably say no when you ask if you can paint your room's walls. But go to them requesting permission to cover a wall with a cloth instead of with paint—and you're home free!

So huddle with your students to choose the design and colors of your "wall" (handprints and first names are favorites), then browse your hardware store for a canvas drop cloth and paint (acrylic latex gloss enamel works well). This low-budget wall hanging will personalize and brighten your room. *Doug Partin*

GREAT GRAPHICS

Promote your activities in a big way or redecorate your youth group room with billboard art. Notice the billboards in your area, and try to think of some creative applications to get your message across. Next, contact your local outdoor advertiser and see if the company will let you look through its stock. Often they will just give you a billboard, or part of one, if they receive a letter from your church stating that it will not be used for any moneymaking venture or commercial advertising. You might also want to offer a donation receipt to the company.

Use the billboard as a wall decoration in your youth group room, as part of a skit, or as a promotion for a particular activity. There are lots or possibilities. *Gary Ogdon*

HAND-PAINTED WALLS

So the bare walls of your new office aren't very stimulating, huh? You don't need *House Beautiful* to brighten up your working environment—just use the hands of your kids and your volunteer teachers.

Tape on the walls whatever patterns you want to be painted. Choose two or three semi-gloss latex paint colors similar in value—that is, one color doesn't overpower the other. Then announce in Sunday school that all students may come to your office (with a teacher, if they are youngsters) and put their handprints on your wall. And beware of the enthusiasm you'll generate!

Let them dip their hands into a paint pan of one of the two or three colors, scrape the excess off on the edge of the pan, and carefully press their hands in two or three different areas of the taped-off portions of the walls. Don't pull their hands off the wall too quickly, or you'll get spatters. According to the students' ages, provide the necessary escort to the wash-up area. And get members of your adult staff to leave their prints, too!

What will you get besides inspiring office walls? First, you'll get to meet most of your kids—an important point if you're new and if you supervise elementary kids. Second, as you sit in your office and let your eyes wander now and then, you can't help but visualize the lives behind those handprints. It just may encourage your prayer time for the kids and adults to whom you minister. *Eric Wooding*

RESOURCES

BOOK SHARING

Encourage reading among people of all ages in the church by simply setting up a library in which books may be traded rather than simply checked out. People may take any book from the library (for keeps if they wish) as long as they trade in another book of comparable value. Although all trading is done by the honor system, appoint someone to oversee the library, handle book swaps, and keep an orderly display. *Al Johnson*

CHRISTIAN TAPE LIBRARY

Since Christian music cassettes and CDs are sometimes too expensive for kids to buy, make them more available to your kids by creating a music library at your church. The kids in your group can purchase a library card for a nominal fee and use it to borrow cassettes or CDs for one week at a time. You can also ask the kids to leave a deposit on each CD to ensure its return. Catalog the tapes and run the whole thing like a lending library. You can have fines for late returns. Some kids may want to buy more than one library card so they can check out more than one CD at a time.

Use the collected money to buy more music. You might be able to get discounts by joining a Christian music club or by buying music on sale at a Christian bookstore or a large music store chain. *Todd Wagner*

COLLEGE CATALOG CORNER

To help your senior highers make decisions about life after high school, contact private and public colleges and vocational technical institutions with a request for their current catalog, admissions, and financial aid information. There is no charge for this service and most schools are eager to reply as well as to pay the return postage.

Then set up a table or corner bookshelf in the senior high room or church library and use a sign-out system to keep track of the catalogs. You can post a sign of guidance that reads, "Expect God to guide, not decide!" This is a great way to inform people about possibilities for their continuing education. *Matt and Janelle Kuntscher*

END ROLLS OF NEWSPRINT

Go to your local newspaper and ask for the end rolls, which are the leftover rolls of newsprint that they print the paper on. There are usually dozens of these available every day which contain lots of paper, good for drawing on, painting on, sketching, or any other creative thing. Each end roll will contain as much as 50 feet of good usable paper.

LIBRARY COURTESY CARDS

If your personal or church library suffers from the disappearing book syndrome, then this idea might help. Print up small cards like the one shown here and ask book borrowers to fill one out when they borrow a book.

The card is not so much for your benefit, however, as it is for your borrowers'. It can be used as a bookmark and as a reminder of their need to return the book. A humorous touch makes it easier to fill out the cards. *Scott Welch*

Fabulous 44 Commandments

If you need some rules for your youth group, try the ones on page 43. Rules will usually go over a little better if they are presented with a sense of humor. Post a copy and distribute them to each member of the group. *Randy Nichols*

Junior-High Ticket Program

Here's a creative way to control the behavior and misbehavior of highly exuberant junior high youth using ordinary, double-rolled tickets. You can usually buy these numbered tickets in local stationery stores, paper supply companies, or party supply stores.

Reward them for good behavior and penalize them for bad behavior in a fun and nonthreatening way.

When kids arrive, they receive five tickets to keep with them throughout the meeting. Place the matching stubs in a container.

Rules for acceptable and unacceptable behavior should be explained to kids ahead of time so that when kids misbehave, they aren't surprised when a leader takes a ticket away from them. Kids can lose tickets at anytime during the meeting, during games, free time, Bible Study, devotions, and anything else that is planned.

Award prizes (candy, soda, etc.) at the end of the meeting by drawing ticket stubs from the container. When a ticket stub is drawn that matches a number of a ticket that has been removed from a kid for misbehavior, choose another stub.

Tell kids to retain all their tickets for six months. Then kids can use those tickets to make bids at an auction for special prizes. This incentive rewards kids for good behavior.

Although difficult discipline problems are not going to be solved with this kind of program, it can help make kids more aware of the fact that their behavior does matter in a group setting. *Steve Christopher*

Youth Group Contract

If discipline is a problem in your youth group, create a Youth Group Contract with the students. At one of your meetings, announce or pass out a list of proposed rules you have chosen in advance. (The more the better. It's good to include a few that border on being ridiculous.) Also ask the kids for their suggestions. When the list is complete, divide the group into smaller units and have them decide which rules they want to keep and which they want to eliminate. They should keep those they feel are fair, just, and necessary for the youth group to run smoothly.

Then have a discussion with the whole group, with each smaller group sharing their conclusions along with their reasons. If you find that the students have eliminated some useful rules or have kept some undesirable ones, you may express your feelings also. But the final decision should be left to a vote of the group. Usually they will do a very good job of selecting or modifying the rules they consider worthwhile and will honor. When all of this is completed, list the rules on a sheet of poster paper or parchment and let everyone sign it at the bottom. Post it on the wall as a reminder that you now have a contract.

Of course, you may need to add amendments as you go along, adding or dropping rules when the group agrees. Some rules may be more important than others. The idea is to predetermine standards for group behavior in advance so that you are never accused of being a dictator when you must administer disciplinary action. Usually this procedure is more useful with large groups than smaller ones. *(From Junior High Ministry by Wayne Rice, Zondervan Publishers, 1978)*

Put-Down Covenant

Put-downs—negative comments made by one person about another—can seriously undermine relationships in a youth group if they're allowed to go unchecked. Here's one way to help stem the tide.

Thus Saith the Youth Pastor...

The Fabulous 44 Commandments
Official Youth Group Rules

There shall be no:

1. fighting
2. biting
3. proselytizing
4. stabbing
5. jabbing
6. grabbing
7. smoking
8. choking
9. poking
10. cussing
11. fussing
12. Robitussing
13. stealing

14. dealing
15. feeling
16. revealing
17. breaking
18. partaking
19. bellyaching
20. leaving
21. cleaving
22. deceiving
23. sneaking
24. reeking
25. streaking
26. scheming
27. screaming
28. blaspheming

29. shaming
30. flaming
31. maiming
32. blaming
33. cutting
34. butting
35. smutting
36. lipping
37. tripping
38. stripping
39. running
40. gunning
41. shunning
42. shooting
43. fruiting

Yes, these really are the rules. But some explanation might be in order. The footnotes may clarify what's expected as a privileged member of our youth group.

• Rules 1, 2, 4, 5, 8, 9, 31, 34, and 39 deal with what is known to wee children as "playing too rough."

• Rules 6, 13, and 17 refer to taking or damaging articles that belong to others or to the church.

• Rule 3 means no selling stuff or trying to get people to join your Herbalife group or any other organization while you are at church or on a youth group activity.

• Rules 7, 12, 14, 18, and 30 indicate that the following are not to be used or distributed and should not be present at any youth activity: cigarettes, lighter or matches, alcoholic beverages, prescription and nonprescription drugs. (If you must take medication, have your parent give it—along with dosage—to the youth pastor prior to the activity.)

• Rules 10, 11, 19, 27, 29, 32, and 41 deal with verbal arguments, fights, slander, and angry remarks to or against others. These are not acceptable. If you have a problem with someone, an adult sponsor will help the two of you work things out.

• Rules 15, 21, and 36 refer to relationships with the opposite sex. Your behavior should be discreet and proper while on church property or at an activity.

• Rules 16, 25, and 38 address acceptable attire for youth group activities. The church dress code should be followed except when differences are announced.

• Rules 20, 22, 23, and 26 mean that if you come to an event, you are expected to remain until the event is over, and then wait in the designated areas of activity until your parent-approved ride picks you up. You are to speak and act with integrity while attending youth group acitivities.

• Rule 24 means you should come to events clean—for the sake of others and yourself.

• Rules 10, 28, and 35 means profanity, vulgarity, and dirty jokes have no place during church activities.

• Rules 33, 40, and 42 means no knives, guns, or other weapons should be brought onto church grounds or to any youth event.

• Rule 43 means that food (fruit) is served to be eaten, not played with or thrown. No food fights.

• Rule 44 doesn't apply to our annual Skydiving-over-Active-Volcanoes fellowship.

Spend some time with the youth group discussing the subject of put-downs and how important it is to be careful about what we say to each other (James 3:2-12).

Following this study, have the kids create a Put-down Covenant similar to the one on page 45. You might pass out a sample, and allow the kids to modify it or add their own thoughts to it. Then have everyone sign it and post it in the meeting room as a constant reminder that put-downs are unacceptable in the youth group by their own agreement. *David C. Wright*

PUT-DOWN POTTY

If you're having trouble with kids who constantly put each other down in youth meetings and activities, try this. Get a child's potty seat and label it the Put-Down Potty. Then, whenever a member of the group (youth or sponsor) puts another person down, the culprit must pay a fine. The fine can be collected in the potty, and the money collected can be sent to a worthy mission project.

This approach calls attention to the problem without being heavy-handed. The increased awareness will result in fewer put-downs. The fine can be set at any level you feel will be most effective and fair to all. *Hal Evans*

OTHER ADMINISTRATION IDEAS

12 COMMANDMENTS OF YOUTH WORK

The following 12 commandments are actually 12 ways to make sure your youth group goes down the drain, but it is a helpful list of no-no's for any good youth worker. You may want to hang them on your office wall.

• **Wipe out incentive.** Tell your kids that someone tried their ideas six years ago. It didn't work then, and it won't work now!

• **Depend on only a few teens.** Use a few pets for every activity and privilege. Don't try to develop responsibility in others.

• **Do not commend your teens.** Take them and their efforts for granted.

• **Reprimand your teens for weaknesses.** Never bother to pray that they will be strengthened. Just scold they for their faults.

• **Expect everyone to conform to your way of thinking.** This covers everything! Whatever might happen...you are always right!

• **Don't try to develop group spirit and morale among your teens.** Why waste precious time developing traits they should have developed long ago?

• **Do not spend time with them personally.** Tell them you are too busy to listen to their problems; besides, you have enough problems of your own.

• **Betray confidences.** Use a confidence given to you by one of your young people as an illustration in your youth meeting.

• **Set up a spy system.** Ask your pets to report any questionable things going on among their friends. It will foster doubt and mistrust (to say nothing of disunity).

• **Blame your failure as a leader on the kids.** We will let you define this point yourself...no one knows better than you who is really to blame.

• **Make Christianity a religion of don'ts.** Be sure to capitalize on all of the no-no's of Christianity. This is much easier than teaching that the Christian life is a healthy, disciplined freedom, offering opportunity for our own self-expression and taking on responsibilities.

• **Be a grump.** No one likes anyone better than an all-around grump. It does wonders for the morale and spirit of the entire group! *Jim Hayford*

STORING POSTERS

What a waste to spend time and energy on that poster only to throw it away after one use, or cram it behind a filing cabinet never to retrieve it again. One way to prevent that from happening is to use clothes pant hangers, the kind with the two spring clasps. You can hang several posters on one hanger. Hang them with the blank sides together so you can easily check front and back to see the two posters. Then you can hang them in an unused closet or use a door hanger and keep them right where you can find them. *Jim Bourne*

MAKING THE GRADE

This program will get raves from your parents, the community, and the media—not to mention build attendance. Provide an hour of tutoring once a week immediately before your Sunday evening or midweek meeting. Recruit competent teachers and other professionals to help your teenagers with

Put-down Covenant

We would like our youth group to be a place where everyone can come, feel accepted, and feel good about themselves.

We know that put-downs and criticisms make people feel rejected, hurt, and bad about themselves.

We also know that hurting others in any way is wrong before God.

Therefore, we promise, with God's help, to:

1. Stop putting others down ourselves with words or actions.

2. Remind others in the group of their responsibility not to put others down.

3. Ask forgiveness from God and from others when we fail.

4. Forgive others when they fail.

Signed   Date

_____   _____

_____   _____

_____   _____

_____   _____

_____   _____

_____   _____

_____   _____

_____   _____

_____   _____

_____   _____

_____   _____

_____   _____

  45

homework and special academic needs. Enhance the program periodically with special classes on how to study, preparing for the SAT, etc.

Not only will your kids appreciate the academic help, but most of them will stay for the following youth meeting. *Bill Splawn*

HAVE TOYS, WILL TRAVEL

If you work with kids, you can turn what might be a potentially boring situation into a lot of fun by always having on hand a suitcase or box in the trunk of your car loaded with games, gimmicks, and miscellaneous fun items. Suggested contents of the box: playing cards, Nerf Balls, Frisbees, marbles, a football, a basketball, rope, Ping-Pong balls, board games, silly soap, and so on. *Dave Bransby*

DO-IT-YOURSELF FOG MACHINE

Make your own dry-ice fog machine, which can be used for all kinds of things: dramatic or musical productions, haunted houses, photo sessions, or whenever you want to create an eerie effect. You'll need the following items:
• A 3- to 5-gallon bucket
• Some heavy-duty cardboard
• An electric hair dryer
• About six feet of dryer vent hose (4" diameter preferred)
• Duct tape
• Hot water and dry ice

You can find all these items, except the ice, at home or at a hardware store. Dry ice outlets are listed in the telephone directory under Ice.

To build your fog machine, place the bucket upside down on the cardboard and trace around it. Cut

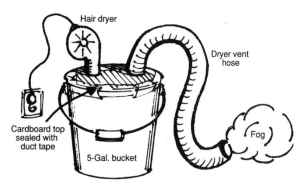

the cardboard to make a lid for the bucket. Next, cut holes in the top of the lid for both the hair dryer nozzle and the dryer vent hose (a little small-

er than the hose, so the hose can be twisted into the hole and will stay). Use duct tape to seal the cardboard lid around the top of the bucket.

When the lid is sealed and the hose attached, you're ready to make fog. Here's how: Fill the bucket about half full (through the hair dryer hole in the top—be careful) with hot water. You might want to use a large funnel to avoid getting water on the cardboard lid. Or you can fill the bucket with hot water before you seal the lid onto the bucket.

Chop dry ice with an ice pick into small pieces to drop through the hair dryer hole. After the ice is in, turn on the hair dryer and place it into the hole. The fan in the hair dryer will force the fog out the other hole, through the hose. Use the hose to direct the fog wherever you want it. The longer your hose, the farther you can spread the fog. It works!

Be sure to wear gloves when handling the dry ice, avoid inhaling the carbon-dioxide fog, and be careful using electric devices (the hair dryer) near water. *Dan Craig*

RUBBER CEMENT SOLUTION

If you have ever tried to get the last half of rubber cement out of the bottle with a dried brush applicator, you know how sticky and difficult it is. Your average underrated pump oil can with

elongated spout makes a terrific applicator. You can neatly distribute the cement where it needs to go. The tip of the spout causes the last of the cement to dry, sealing the rest for smooth use all the way to the last drop. *Jim Bourne*

HANGING POSTERS

The old cliche, "There's a right way and a wrong way to do anything," even applies to hanging posters. Put a flat piece of masking tape on the back of each corner. Then attach little roll of tape

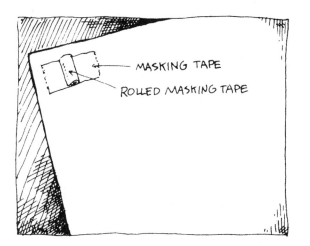

MASKING TAPE
ROLLED MASKING TAPE

directly on the first piece of tape rather than on the poster, and you won't tear the poster when you take it down. *Jim Bourne*

ON THE ROAD AGAIN

Whether en route to a distant location, extended bus trips can either break your back or build relationships and provide ministry to the travelers. Here are some ways to make bus trips work for you instead of against you.

• **Count off!** Assign everyone a number at the beginning of the trip; whenever attendance must be taken, the kids simply count off instead of you hollering out names five times a day. (Challenge your group to top their best time for counting off!)

• **No more paper-thin sandwiches.** Save bag lunches from being mashed into every nook in the bus by storing them all in a large cooler.

• **Rolling library.** After a few days they'll tire of Uno and the fifteen handheld computer games. So when you hear them wind up for another round of "Father Abraham," quick—get out some books you packed along just for this moment and pass them out. Anything from Pilgrim's Progress to Garfield is fair game.

• **Home, sweet home.** Let the kids personalize the bus with memorabilia garnered along the trip—after all, it makes the vehicle homey and builds group identity and memories. Remember to pack a few rolls of tape.

• **Prizes! Prizes!** Keep an eye open for special "achievements" that you can capitalize on at the trip's end: the AT&T User Appreciation Award (for most time spent calling home);

the Kleenex Three-Boxer Award (for the most homesick); the Tiny Bladder Award (for most potty stops requested); etc.

• **Pick a seat, any seat.** Extended bus trips can be valuable interactive experiences. Teenagers, however, are vicious creatures of habit and territory. If left to their own devices, they are notorious for gravitating to the back of the bus while the timid junior highers get bulldozed (if not launched) to the front. Couples, meanwhile, disappear below the tops of the seat backs. You can stir things up occasionally by beginning the day with a novel seating assignment, thereby putting people next to others who they would never have chosen to sit with.

Let these kindle your creativity:

Revelation 22:13 Day. Because Jesus is the Alpha and the Omega, everyone sits in alphabetical order.

Matthew 19:30 Day. Because the first shall be last, and the last shall be first, those in the back of the bus must swap with those in the front).

Genesis 1:27 Day. Females and males on opposite sides of the aisle.
David Shaw

CHEAPO LIMO

Have you ever wanted to give one or more of your kids a limo ride as a prize for winning a contest or to recognize a special achievement of some kind? Unfortunately, they're a tad expensive.

You can enjoy the luxury of a limo without the high cost by borrowing an older model Lincoln or Cadillac (a full-sized four-door with a big back seat) and adding a battery-powered TV, a cellular phone, a bottle of sparkling cider, some classical music on the tape deck, and a chauffeur (the youth pastor).

Drive the kids around town, take pictures, make a big deal out of it—the kids will love it.
Roger Rome

APPRECIATION FILE

Get extra encouragement out of those seldom-received notes of appreciation by putting them in a personal file. Over the months and years the file grows, and on days when you feel that no one appreciates your efforts, you can flip through this file to see and remind yourself of what your young people, parents, and coworkers really think of you. *Tim Lighthall*

CARAVAN CONTROL

No youth worker who transports lots of kids in several vehicles can relax entirely until everyone's home safely—not one lost or hurt in an accident. The guidelines on page 49 can make caravanning a safe and efficient procedure. Make plenty of copies to give to drivers at each event.

One last detail—always include clear directions to your destination, so that if the caravan vehicles are separated, everyone will get there sooner or later. *Ted Stecher*

Caravan Control

1. Drive safely.

2. Drive with your headlights on.

3. If there is a mechanical difficulty, blink your lights off and on. This signal should be relayed to the first vehicle in line; all vehicles should then try to pull off the road and stop as soon as possible.

4. If your vehicle's fuel drops below ___ tank, turn on your hazard blinkers. The entire caravan should stop at the next service station.

5. Stay in line—do not pass.

6. Maximum speed is 55 m.p.h. unless conditions call for slower going. We cannot go faster than the slowest vehicle.

7. Stay in sight—do not lag behind or get too far ahead.

8. If you cannot keep up, turn your headlights off and your hazard blinkers on. (If you're driving at night turn your headlights from low beam to high beam repeatedly.) This signal should be relayed to the front vehicle so that the speed can be adjusted accordingly.

Caravan Control

1. Drive safely.

2. Drive with your headlights on.

3. If there is a mechanical difficulty, blink your lights off and on. This signal should be relayed to the first vehicle in line; all vehicles should then try to pull off the road and stop as soon as possible.

4. If your vehicle's fuel drops below ___ tank, turn on your hazard blinkers. The entire caravan should stop at the next service station.

5. Stay in line—do not pass.

6. Maximum speed is 55 m.p.h. unless conditions call for slower going. We cannot go faster than the slowest vehicle.

7. Stay in sight—do not lag behind or get too far ahead.

8. If you cannot keep up, turn your headlights off and your hazard blinkers on. (If you're driving at night turn your headlights from low beam to high beam repeatedly.) This signal should be relayed to the front vehicle so that the speed can be adjusted accordingly.

PUBLICITY

Don't merely ask for people's attention—capture it! Here are new ways to use the good ol' announcements, fliers, calendars, direct mail, and posters. Cases in point: list your schedule of activities in *TV Guide* format (page 63). Design a narrow poster for your next event that fits on the inside of a locker door (84). Or buy ad space in the high school student newspaper (96).

ANNOUNCEMENTS

PROPHETIC ADVERTISING

Instead of the standard promotional material on your next event, create a prophetic news article about how it will happen. Include all information

about the event in the news clipping. Write it up like a news article taken from the local newspaper, using as many details as possible. To stir up some curiosity, add some names and descriptions of what could occur. *Len Cuthbert*

AND NOW FOR THE ANNOUNCEMENTS

Those words put most listeners to sleep. Wake your group up with shockingly creative announcements like these:

• Tape sign-up sheets under all the seats. Attach a dollar bill to one or two of the sheets. Or attach stickers to a couple of sign-up sheets; sticker-holders may go to the front to claim a prize.

• Dress up a high schooler in an ice-hockey goalie's uniform to make the announcement.

• Is the announcement for your adult congregation? Dress a high schooler up like a pizza-delivery guy and run him up to the pulpit during announcements with a pizza for the pastor. When the delivery person appears to realize what church this is, he asks the pastor why he's ordering out for pizza when his own youth group is taking orders for a fundraising pizza sale.

• Play a tape recording of the announcement while the announcement giver lip syncs it. With practice, she can mouth the words just out of sync enough with the recording so that it looks even more curious, like an old Japanese or Italian movie.

• Advertising an event? Hold a handful of balloons by their strings and for every excuse that you imag-

ine students would give for not attending the event, pop a balloon. End the announcement with "If you don't come, you'll burst my bubble."
• Tape candy to fliers, and then throw them out to the students.
• Play Guy Smiley, the game-show host. Say, "Next week's event is full of surprises. Tell them what to expect, Bob." Then over the sound system, an off-camera voice—like the game show voice that describes the prizes—announces the event.
• Push into the room public enemy number one of youth group events: a TV. Read from *TV Guide* what programs are on the night of the event, including the synopses and actors. Then state that all programs will be taped and replayed after the event for the benefit of students.
• Before the meeting set out an easy chair and an end table; on the table set a lamp and a drink. At an appropriate time during the meeting, a student in a bathrobe or smoking jacket meanders in, settles himself in the chair, and makes the announcement.
• A drama student can mime an announcement.
• A small group can divide into teams and play charades in order to get your announcement across.
• Deliver your announcement in rap.
• During busy seasons with several events to promote, bring a bagful of items that will visually remind your group of the events: a combination lock (lock-in), ski goggles (ski trip), Christmas ornament (Christmas party), CD case (Christian concert), hammer (service project). The second week you announce these events, all you'll have to do is pull the objects from the bag—Santa's bag, if it's December—and the kids will shout back to you the event.

Now you create some! *Clay Nelson and Tom Daniel*

THE VANISHING OPPORTUNITY

Your kids may perk up during announcement time after you try this idea on them.

Hold up a piece of paper with your announcement written boldly on it. As you display it to them, end your brief advertising spiel with something like "...and don't forget to sign up next Sunday. After that, your opportunity to attend this event will be gone," at which point you pull a lighter from your pocket and ignite the sheet of paper, tossing it into the air at the same time. It will flame up and totally disappear in a flash.

The trick is accomplished by using flash paper that can be purchased in a magician's supply or novelty shop. Don't try it with regular paper or you're liable to burn down the church. Flash paper is safe and grabs the kids' attention. *David Parke*

PIZZA PARADE

With a dictionary or thesaurus—and some alliterative knack—you can create some fun announcements for events, or even the events themselves. Here's a sample letter that was sent to one youth group:

Dear group member,
You and your peers are invited to a Pizza Parade.
    "What in the pink pizzazz is a Pizza Parade?" you ask.
A Pizza Parade is—
• Plenty of pizzas of all proportions properly prepared by prominent persons of perfectly pompous prestige.
• Properly praised pizza in a picturesque and palatable presentation.
• A pleasant way to playfully petition you to prepare and participate in a popular and poetic project promoting a proper perspective and the Prince of Peace.
    "Sounds pretty peppy, not to mention powerful," you pronounce, and you are precisely perfect in your prediction.
    Preregister for this party by October 10 with the paltry pile of two dollars.
    "Preposterous!" you say. Perhaps. But for you to partake in this particular pizza production, we press you to persuade your parents, pull in your peers, and present your person in either purple or pink.
    Proudly practicing persuasion,
    Gwen

Kimberly Weast

NEWSLETTER SEARCH

If your young people tend to take your group's newsletter or printed announcements for granted, try this. Announce that you'll distribute your next newsletter differently in order to save on postage. Then tell kids to bring a flashlight to the youth meeting.

Before the meeting address all your newsletters as usual, but hide them all over the church. Put them in hard-to-find places, but keep track of where each person's newsletter is. When the kids arrive, they must search for their newsletters in a dimly lit church. If they find another's newsletter, they are to leave it where they found it.

Give prizes to the first people to find their newsletters and booby prizes to those who are last or who fail to find them at all. Following the search, read the newsletter together to emphasize those things that are important. *Mark A. Simone*

CD ANNOUNCEMENT

To promote your group's activities, first come up with a name that sounds like a band or music group. Then create a CD insert that looks like the real thing, complete with outrageous pictures of the band—the youth group

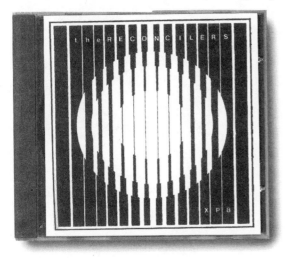

leaders. Buy CD covers or buy or create plastic sleeves to look like CD holders. Instead of a CD, place a calendar inside that details upcoming events. Or fill the CD holder with brochures, fliers, or leaflets about your group's activities. The kids will love it. *Mark Thompson*

ANNOUNCEMENT COMPETITION

Do your young people have a hard time remembering upcoming events? Fortify their memories and have fun at the same time with this idea.

For announcement time at your next meeting, divide the group into teams and give each team an announcement that needs to be made. Give each

team some poster board, marking pens, and other supplies that might come in handy.

In five minutes each team must create an appealing announcement. It can be a poster, commercial, skit, song, cheer—anything they can create. Give an award to the group that does the best job.

With such an approach, creativity is stimulated, the announcements are effective, and the kids are much less likely to forget what's happening. *Michael Berry*

ANNOUNCEMENT TREASURE HUNT

Divide the group into small hunting teams, and give each team a 3x5 index card with one or more facts about the upcoming event, as well as a clue that reveals where they'll find the next card.

Each group gets a different set of cards with a different announcement printed on them. When each group has all its cards, kids can then get all the facts arranged in the proper order and make the announcement to the rest of the group.

This game can also be done as a relay with one person per group chasing down each new card and then returning to the group. It adds a lot of fun and excitement to announcements and helps fight those age-old excuses: "I forgot" and "I didn't know about that." *Michael Berry*

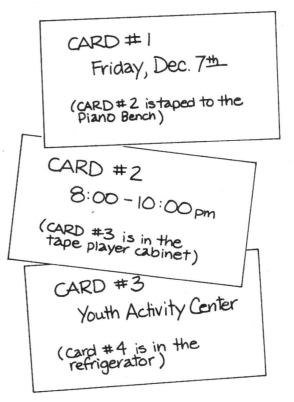

ANNOUNCEMENT CHARADES

If you have a large group and lots of announcements to make, try this. Divide your group into small teams of four or five kids each.

Give each team one or two announcements written on 3x5 index cards. Teams have three minutes to create a charade that will allow the others to guess the announcement. Give a prize to the team with the most creative and effective approach. If all of the announcements are about the same in length and difficulty, divide into two teams and play by regular charade rules, timing the charades and awarding a prize to the fastest team. It's a surefire way to get your kids involved in the announcements. *Mike Young*

PUZZLED ANNOUNCEMENTS

Think up various kinds of word puzzles that have as their answers the details of coming events. Many types of puzzles will work—crosswords, etc. Copy them and pass them out at the end of the meeting, and the kids must figure out the puzzle to know what is coming up. Post a completed puzzle later on—just in case. *Ken Owen*

ACTION ANNOUNCEMENTS

Before the meeting begins, write all the announcements that need to be made on little slips of paper. Then, go through them and think of an unusual but appropriate method of presenting each announcement. This could be pantomime, poetry (making the announcement into a rhyme), a news report, an interview, a song, alternating words (two individuals read the announcement by each reading every other word), charades, and so on. You will also need to mark on each slip the number of participants required for each one. Here's a sample of how an announcement slip might be written:

> Pantomime - One Person
>
> Car Wash
> This Saturday at the Church
> 10 a.m to 4 p.m.

Then at the meeting, ask for volunteers. You don't have to tell them what they will be doing. Try to match the various methods of presenting the announcements with teens who you know will be able to pull them off. Then send all the volunteers out of the room for five minutes or so to prepare their announcement. (An adult sponsor could accompany them to give instructions and help.) During this time you can do something else with the rest of the group. Then call the volunteers back in and let them do their thing. *Darrel Johnson*

WILD PITCH

Here's a good way to advertise the beginning of your church's softball season (if your church is into that) or any other event that you might want to advertise with a baseball theme. Cut a baseball in half with a power saw, and then

attach one side of the baseball to each side of a window. It will appear as if the ball is stuck in the glass. It should be located in a heavily traveled area of the church where people will see it. You can also paint some cracks around the ball to make it look more authentic.

Under the ball you can put your announcement, sign-up list, or whatever. With a little creativity, you could use this attention-getter for all kinds of announcements: a spring training seminar, a sales pitch, a good way to have a ball, and so on. *Mike Leamnson*

COMMANDMENT CARDS

Here's how to make customized get well or announcement cards that you can print yourself on plain or construction paper folded business-letter style. On the front draw a picture of Moses or stone tablets and print the words, "It is written, 'Thou shalt' . . . " Leave space underneath to complete the message, such as "come to youth group" or "pay your camp bill."

Inside the first fold you can print, "Where is it written, you ask?" Inside the second fold print, "Page one of this card!" Below that is more space for specific details or a personal message. *Don Warner*

HOW TO EVADE A DATE

Announce your next youth event with this skit. Irwin the nerd calls Susan for a date. He is nervous and awkward during the conversation, but he's determined to get a date. Susan, desperate for reasons to refuse, uses the youth group calendar for convenient excuses—each excuse, of course, being an announcement of an actual upcoming event for your group. Using the script on pages 58-59, just replace Susan's excuses with your own group's upcoming events. As usual, hamming it up adds to the fun. *Doug Mathers*

DINNER THEATER

This three-skit series was used to promote a Valentine's Day youth group dinner theater. You can adapt the three skits on pages 60-62 to fit your own special occasion. *Doug Mathers*

Student Ministries Present

The Calvary Dinner Theater

6:45-9:30 on the evenings of
February 14 and 16
Tickets: $9.50 per person

Please join us for an evening of culinary delight and theatrical merriment. An impeccable evening to venerate your Valentine sentiments.

Le Menu

Poulet grille
Riz melange (sauvage et domestique)
Haricots verts aux champignons
Cerises supreme
Lait
Cafe

For reservations: Please call 282-4612, or put a check in the offering plate (please note the event in the memo for the convenience of our ushers).
Dress code: Please dress as ostentatiously—gaudily—as possible. Put on those ties, prom dresses, and costume jewelry. Sequins are encouraged.
Ticket Reservations
Name of party: _____
Number in party: _____
Date of reservations: _____
Phone number: _____
All proceeds will be used to support our summer mission trip to the Dominican Republic.

HOW TO EVADE A DATE

CAST
•Narrator •Irwin •Susan

Scene: *Irwin, stage left, is dressed in the latest nerd look. Susan, chewing gum and wearing a cheerleading outfit, stands with her back to the audience at stage right.*

NARRATOR: February has begun, and within this auspicious month lurks a holiday that puts us all in the mood for love. Yes, I'm talking about President's Day—I mean St. Valentine's Day. While we all enjoy the thought of romance, you probably don't go out with just anyone who calls. As a service to those of you who must plot ways of getting out of a date, we now present to you a brief educational drama called "How to Evade a Date."

IRWIN: *(nervously rubbing his palms together as he works up courage to make a phone call)* Eight-three-one-four-five-seven-eight. One ring, two ri—Hello? This is Irwin. Do you want to go out with me this Friday night? Oh...sorry, Mr. Vanity...uh, is Irwin there? I mean, is Miss Susan Vanity there? Yes sir, I'll hold.

SUSAN: *(enters calling over her shoulder in a sickeningly sweet voice)* Okay, Daddy. I'll get it on my own phone. (picks up receiver) Hello?

IRWIN: Hello. Is this Susan Vanity?

SUSAN: Yes.

IRWIN: Hi, Susan. This is Irwin Testube. I'm in your biology class.

SUSAN: *(obviously not recognizing who Irwin is)* Yes?

IRWIN: I sit right in front of you...*(awkward pause)*...you copy my answers during tests.

SUSAN: *(nervously clearing her throat)* Yes, I know who you are now.

IRWIN: Well, I was wondering, Susan, if you'd like to go to a movie with me this Friday night? Return of the Nerds is showing at Cinemax for only a dollar.

SUSAN: Oh, I'd love to, Irwin, but I have to...to...*(looks frantically around her room, sees the trash can, reaches in and pulls out a crumpled youth group calen-*

dar)...I have to go to a junior high progressive dinner with my church. It starts at six and goes until almost midnight. But it would have really been fun. Sorry, but—

IRWIN: But you're in senior high.

SUSAN: I know, Irwin, but I promised to...uh...help with the dishes.

IRWIN: How about joining me on Saturday, February 24? There's a really swell exhibit at the science museum on the reproductive rituals of African elephants.

SUSAN: Well, that does sound interesting, but I...**(still flipping through calendar)**...I'll be gone that whole weekend on a retreat up in northern Minnesota with my senior high youth group—you know, skiing, horseback riding, playing broomball, cheering the snow-football players.

IRWIN: Well, what about Wednesday, the 14th? I hear there's an Elvis look-alike contest at the mall.

SUSAN: Sorry. Gotta go to church and make sure I pay my deposit for the retreat by that night. And every Wednesday I have youth group.

IRWIN: How about Tuesday?

SUSAN: Uh, Tuesdays...no, I use Tuesdays to wash my hair so I look my best for youth group.

IRWIN: Sunday night?

SUSAN: No good. Small groups at—

SUSAN AND IRWIN: (in unison) church.

IRWIN: How does March look?

SUSAN: Well, I don't have that calendar yet, but I know that there is a junior high retreat I'll need to pray for and a senior high progressive dinner on the 17th. Boy, I'm afraid I'm pretty booked up.

IRWIN: You know, all that stuff is beginning to sound fun. Maybe I can come with you for some of them.

SUSAN: Sorry, Irwin, I've got to go...I hear your mother calling. 'Bye, and thanks for calling. **(hangs up)**

IRWIN: (looking at phone) Boy, is she ever religious. And I wonder why my mother was calling her?

END

Copyright Youth Specialties, 1224 Greenfield Dr., El Cajon, CA 92021.

DINNER THEATER

Promo Skit One

A couple who not only talk loudly but also dress loudly, Mr. and Mrs. Loud are each dressed in clashing polyester clothing. Mr. Loud's hair is slicked down, and Mrs. Loud wears a flowered hat and cat-eye glasses. They remind you of how the Beverly Hillbillies might dress for a fancy occasion. Both speak in a very loud drawl. The couple enter the sanctuary late, walking down the center aisle until they get to the front. They then turn to face the congregation and continue talking very loudly to each other.

MR. LOUD: *(yelling)* Let's sit back here in case the preacher sprays when he preaches—I forgot my handkerchief today.

MRS. LOUD: *(in an equally loud voice)* Iam Loud, how many times do I have to tell you that I like being up front? I want to hear the choir. If they aren't too good, maybe we'll join. I can sing in one of them purty robes. If he's a sprayer, I'll give you some Kleenex. *(pulls out her Kleenex and, blowing her nose loudly, fills the Kleenex—which she hands to Iam)*

MR. LOUD: This shur is a big fancy church. *(fumbling with the bulletin, inserts flying)* Look how much stuff is in their bulletin. I like this church. Now I'll always have paper to doodle on during the preachin'!

MRS. LOUD: Let me see that. Wow, they even got colored paper in here! Look at this. *(reading slowly and with difficulty)* "Student Ministries present"—that must be a fancy name for a youth group—"Student Ministries present the Calvary Dinner Theatre, 6:45 to 9:30, February 14 and 16." That's on Valentine's Day and the Saturday after, ain't it? "Tickets, $9.50 per person."

MR. LOUD: I spend more than that at Baker's Square!

MRS. LOUD: Yeah, but you eat half a pie for dessert.

MR. LOUD: Well, you eat the other half.

MRS. LOUD: *(continuing to read, loudly and laboriously)* "Please join us for an evening of cul...culi...culiflower...no, that ain't it...cul-i-na-ry delight and theehatrical merriment."

MR. LOUD: What does that mean?

MRS. LOUD: It means there'll be skits and stuff after the dinner. *(slowly, feeling her way through the syllables)* "An impeccable evening to venerate your Valentine sentiments."

MR. LOUD: They gonna venerate their Valentine sentiments right here at church?!

MRS. LOUD: *(hitting him with her purse)* I'll venerate my Valentine sentiments!

MR. LOUD: Does it say what they're gonna eat?

MRS. LOUD: *(reading)* "Le Menu, Poulet Grille."

MR. LOUD: That must be the cook—Paulet Griller.

MRS. LOUD: "Rits Melanj, Harry cots verts ox champ...champ-pig-nons."

MR. LOUD: What is that stuff?

MRS. LOUD: I don't know what this hairy cots is, but I think they're gonna serve the champion pig.

MR. LOUD: Oh, boy!

MRS. LOUD: "For reservations, please call 282-4612, or put a check into the offering plate."

MR. LOUD: They always want a check in the offering plate.

MRS. LOUD: Honey, can we go to this-here dinner theater?

MR. LOUD: Why sure, Sugar Lumpkins.

MRS. LOUD: Oh, there's even sumthin' here about what to wear. *(reading)* "Dress code: please dress as ostentashuslee and gawdlely—as possible. Put on those ties, prom dresses, and costume jewelry. Sequins are encouraged."

MR. LOUD: *(leaving with his wife)* I just hope we have something to wear. It's so hard to be ostentashus.

DINNER THEATER

Promo Skit two

Mr. and Mrs. Megabucks are richly dressed, Mr. Megabucks perhaps with a hat and cane and unlit pipe in his mouth, and Mrs. Megabucks with a sequined purse, a fur, hat, white gloves, lots of costume jewelry. Their speech should be slow, loud, and haughty (think of Mr. and Mrs. Thurston Howell the Third from "Gilligan's Island"). Ham it up. They enter talking and walk down the center aisle until they reach the front of the sanctuary behind the microphone.

MRS. MEGABUCKS: It's really so difficult to find a church worthy of our attendance.

MR. MEGABUCKS: I know exactly what you mean, my dear. Not a single BMW or Porsche in the parking lot. But there were certainly a lot of those...

MR & MRS. MEGABUCKS: *(disdainfully, in unison)*...mini-vans!

MRS. MEGABUCKS: I was furthermore disappointed with the doorman. Far too friendly. I like my help to be seen, not heard. They really should purchase uniforms for those men. Those little badges they wear that say "Greeter" on them—they give me a dreadful feeling of equality with the doormen.

MR. MEGABUCKS: The absence of a valet service certainly strikes two points against us coming here.

MRS. MEGABUCKS: Yes, it was appalling to have to walk in from the parking lot.

MR. MEGABUCKS: *(perusing the bulletin and inserts)* As I examine this newsletter, I fail to notice any mention of a men's polo club or even a racquetball club.

MRS. MEGABUCKS: Darling, you don't play racquetball, and you're allergic to horses.

MR. MEGABUCKS: Not the point, my dear. The lack of these two very fine forms of entertainment only emphasizes the absence of elegance—an absence that violates our sense of refinement. Not to mention that attending this church would certainly diminish our social status.

MRS. MEGABUCKS: There does appear to be one exception, Darling. Hand me that colored insert. *(reading)* "Student Ministries present the Calvary Dinner Theatre."

MR. MEGABUCKS: Now, there's a prestigious group.

MRS. MEGABUCKS: Yes, and it appears that they're sponsoring a truly cultural event. Listen to this..."The dinner is to be on the evenings of February 14 and 16. Tickets are only $9.50."

MR. MEGABUCKS: Excellent planning. We can justify the expenditure as an investment in our love.

MRS. MEGABUCKS: How romantic! *(continues reading)* "Please join us for an evening of culinary delight and theatrical merriment."

MR. MEGABUCKS: By Jove, I could use some culinary delight—and I certainly enjoy the theater. I wonder if they'll be doing Shakespeare?

MRS. MEGABUCKS: Oh, wouldn't that be grand? "An impeccable evening to venerate your Valentine sentiments."

MR. MEGABUCKS: The very words I was thinking, my dear.

MRS. MEGABUCKS: Oh, the food sounds absolutely divine.

MR. MEGABUCKS: Read the menu, my dear.

MRS. MEGABUCKS: I can't. It's in French.

MR. MEGABUCKS: In French! Simply elegant!

MRS. MEGABUCKS: And look, they've even put in a dress code for the commoners.

MR. MEGABUCKS: Very open minded of that Student Ministries group. I find myself actually eager to mix some with the lower classes.

MRS. MEGABUCKS: This church may keep us from the horrible arrogance that is sooo prevalent in our world today.

MR. MEGABUCKS: Thank God we're not snobs, my dear. *(both exit)*

DINNER THEATER

Promo Skit three

Iam Lonely, an unsuccessful dating specialist, is a nerd and looks it, complete with taped glasses, white shirt (half untucked), mussed hair, a plethora of pens in his pockets, flared pants, etc. The leader or a student introduces Iam with words to this effect: "This morning we have a special announcement from dating specialist Iam Lonely."

IAM: *(awkwardly, nervously approaches the microphone, stumbling as he reaches it and almost knocking it over)* One, two, three...testing...one, two three...is this thing working? It is? Oh, good...My name is Iam Lonely, the world's foremost authority on first dates. I have had more first dates than anyone on earth. Unfortunately, I haven't had any second dates yet.

Many of you think going to a movie is a good first date. Incorrect. First of all, the popcorn is far too expensive. Secondly, your date may compare you with the actors on the screen and drop you like a hot potato. *(defensively)* Now don't think that this has ever happened to me, personally, but, uh, it has happened to some of my closest friends.

Others prefer to go bowling on their first date. The bowling alley, however, is not a good place to strike the match of love either. Reason number one: you may embarrass yourself with a low score. *(This has not been my problem; I have a 68-pin average.)* Reason number two: your date may be embarrassed. I believe this to be the case with many of my dates. For some reason, they never want to be seen in public. I've concluded this is because of their poor bowling skills. Reason number three: your thumb may become lodged in the ball and you may find yourself sliding down the alley right into the pins. This sporting moment is not a pleasant one; although when this very event transpired on a recent first date, my ball and I scored a strike. Nevertheless, I contend that those who go bowling for a first date are headed straight for the gutter.

"So," you ask, "what is a good first date?" I'm glad you asked. Please locate the pink insert in your bulletin. It gives you the details of not only the best first date, but *(speaking to those who have already articulated your nuptial vows)* the best evening to rekindle the romance in your marriages.

Please read this carefully with me.

"   Student ministries present the Calvary Dinner Theater." A dinner theater is an appropriate dating environment. It provides one with ample opportunity for conversation, as well as entertaining diversions for those times when one lacks subject matter for discussion.

"Six forty-five p.m. to 9:30 p.m., February 14 and 16." That is this Thursday and Saturday. Another reason to commend the dinner theater for your first date is that I have found that it's always a good idea to have a second alternative to your initial request. By the time your potential date thinks of an excuse not to go with you on Thursday, you can spring Saturday on her. Because it is difficult to think of two legitimate excuses within 30 seconds, you'll probably snag your potential date for one of those evenings.

"Tickets are $9.50 per person." This is a genuine bargain. A movie and McDonald's (a terrible first date, by the way), approaches $15 per person, if you go dutch (which I recommend for first dates. No sense investing in a possibly dead-end relationship). The dinner theater price of $9.50 per ticket is far less than I had to pay for repair of the bowling-alley lane.

I trust you will read on in this insert about the food and entertainment yourself.

Note especially the bottom of the insert, which explains how to make reservations: "For reservations please call 282-4612." That's the church number. And when you call, a very pleasant secretary will ask you for the information that you see on the bottom of your insert. Please do not ask the secretary out. She is married (a startling fact, in view of her ignoring my first-date advice).

Another method of registering is to simply fill out the form you are now looking at and turn it in to the office, or place it in the offering plate.

Finally, I would like to say a word about blind dates. I have found that blind dates are one of the most effective ways to get a date. I myself am nearsighted, an impairment that helps conversation inestimably. Just be careful not to step on your date's cat.

That's all the advice for today. Make your reservations soon, and happy dating.

END

LOOKING UP

Here's another way to get the attention of your kids for announcements. Thumb tack or tape your announcements or posters to the ceiling. You can put them anywhere—in the hallways, youth room, or wherever the students congregate. Once someone starts looking up, pretty soon the whole group will. *Robert Garris*

CALENDARS

FRISBEE PUBLICITY

Printing your summer activities calendar on a Frisbee is a unique way to get the information into the hands of your kids—so they don't lose it! You might find a local company to produce this informational Frisbee, or you can contact Custom Ad Design in Ohio at 1-800-899-1620 or at http://www.ourworld.compuserve.com/homepages/jccowan.

No camera-ready artwork is required. *Jay Firebaugh*

WHITE-BOARD CALENDAR

Here's how to make a monthly calendar board that's as fun to create as it is to look at: First, get a large white board. Then purchase thin, colored tape to use as striping. Use the striping to divide the board into 35 squares, like a calendar—seven across and five down.

Use dry-ink pens to mark the dates and events that you've planned for the month. Attach clip art, photos, and other articles to make the board even more colorful and interesting.

Place the board where everyone can see it, including parents. It will attract a lot of attention, and—because it's erasable—you can use it over and over again. *Steve Redmond*

TV GUIDE ANNOUNCEMENT

Print a little booklet that looks like *TV Guide* or your local newspaper's television booklet. All of your upcoming activities and meetings for each month can be listed like TV shows. A little creative writing and a sense of humor will make this idea a winner with your kids. *Ray Wilson*

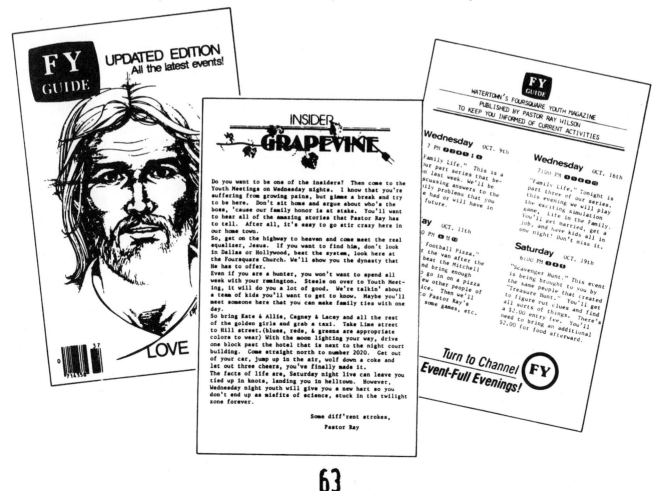

SPIRAL CALENDAR

The shape isn't the only curiosity about this monthly or quarterly activity calendar. Take a closer look at it; between the events are whimsical one-liners that mention the names of the kids in your group.

As you can see from the diagram, start with 15 or so concentric circles; when you fill the outermost circle with words, erase a segment of the circle in order to form a door to the next circle, etc. The effect is dizzying, yet kids will read it to the end if for no other reason than to catch all the quips and see if their names are mentioned. And with some clever scissors work, kids can make unique mobiles to hang in their rooms. *Marty Young.*

A HEAD FOR THE SUMMER CALENDAR

Members of one youth group put their heads together about how to publicize their summer program—and decided that their heads were the very place for it! Call the same screen printers that print T-shirts and ask if they also print on painter caps. Most will. If no one locally does, call American Mills in Minnesota at 1-800-876-4287 for prices and a catalogue.

After you get a reasonable quote, use a laser printer to print out your summer schedule. Then take the printout—plus your youth group's logo and some clip art—to the screen printer. The painter caps imprinted with your group's logo and summer schedule make great publicity—and kids love wearing them during the summer too. *Jay Firebaugh*

CALENDAR WATER BOTTLE

Quench your kids' thirst for summertime activity by printing your summer calendar on water or sport bottles for distribution or sale among your group members.

Whatever you usually print on a calendar sheet—names and times of programs, parties, retreats, studies—simply have it printed on the bottles. Throw in some colorful graphics coordinated with the colors of the bottle and screw-on lid. Include a special youth group name and then make the bottles available to visitors as well as regulars at the beginning of your summer program.

A few phone calls to screen printers in your area will get you started. Otherwise, contact http://www.targetgroup.com/mca/water/ultra.htm.
Jay Firebaugh

YOUTH GROUP COUPON BOOK

Here's an alternative to the annual activity calendar. Print up a coupon book that contains coupons for every event of the year. Some of the coupons can simply be announcements, but others can be for discounts on camp registration and similar events. For certain events include extra coupons that can be used as handouts for friends. Design these like real coupons, using clip art, fancy borders, etc. *Lyle Griner*

POCKET CALENDAR

Design a brightly colored pocket calendar that contains all the upcoming dates of both church and youth activities. It helps prevent a lot of local

Total length 9 inches (folds into 2.5" x 3.5")

church programming conflicts and keeps kids, youth advisors, and parents posted on what's going on.
George Murray

CRAZY CAPERS

To liven up your monthly newsletter or calendar, just slip in a few phony events. Among the serious stuff, insert a ridiculous, impossible event that might fake someone out for a few seconds when they first read it. If nothing else, it will cause students to pay more attention to your communications. It can add some spark and enthusiasm to your group as they anticipate your next crazy caper. Here are a couple examples:

• Sunday, June 31: Over-Night Field Trip to Iceberg, Texas. Tour of the petrified Iceberg Museum; leave church at 12 noon and return when gas is available; bring one VISA card and all the enemies you want.

• Saturday, August 18.5: Sky Diving in Hines Park. Bring chute (or reinforced umbrella) and a sack lunch; meet at church (for prayer). Transportation provided by Schrader's Funeral Home and Traffic Copter 95. We're ready when you are. *John Elliott*

CANNED PUBLICITY

Print activity calendars as labels to be glued to real aluminum cans (see below). Purchase empty cans from a local packing plant for a nominal cost. You might be able to get them with removable lids, enabling the cans to double as banks for saving money for the events.

Display all the cans in your youth group meeting, stacked as if on grocery store shelves, and then distribute them to all the kids. Chances are that these announcements won't get lost as so many do when kids take them home. *David Gilbert*

FLIERS

CAN YOU HEAR A PIN DROP?

To publicize a youth bowling party, bowling-pin-shaped fliers on page 66 with the message "Can you hear a pin drop?" Include the date, time, and location. Put the bowling in an envelope marked LISTEN CAREFULLY in the upper left corner. *Dave Coryell*

FOOTBALL CARDS

This idea is good for outreach, relations with local schools, and group identification. Every fall print up wallet-sized football schedules for the local high school, using the school colors. On the

back put information about your youth group, a phone number kids can call, and perhaps a simple plan of salvation. Make these cards available for the schools to distribute, and for your kids to give to friends. *Bobbi Cordy*

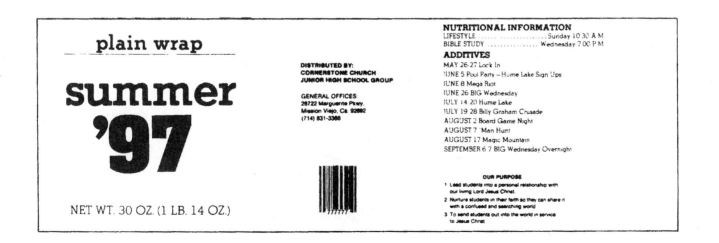

65

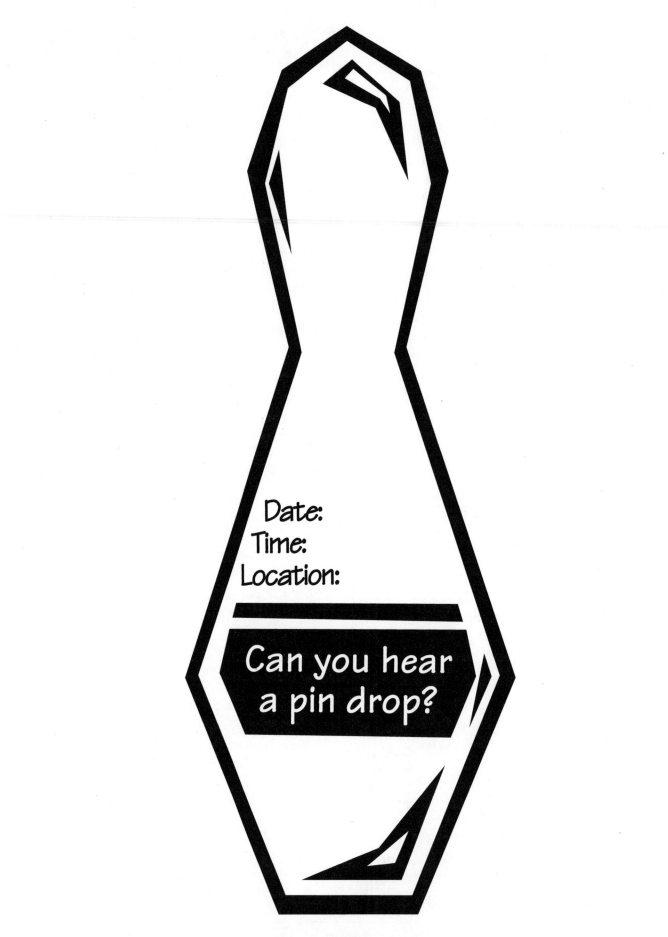

Date:
Time:
Location:

Can you hear a pin drop?

YOUTH GROUP BOOK COVERS

To promote your youth group, print up some attractive book covers for your kids' textbooks. Come up with a design that your kids like for the front, and print your youth group's name and logo on the back. Print enough for youth group kids to give to their friends at school as well. *Robert Crosby*

PIZZA PROMOTION

Here's an idea for a pizza party flier:

Olive you are invited to

Pizza night

on Tuesday, Nov. 11th 6:30 - 8:00
Meat at the church
Dough not forget to **fork** out $2.00.
There is **mushroom** for everyone, so you can bring a friend!
If anyone **sa-uce** they would want to **ham**-ing it up, join us.
We're **bacon** you to come, because any way you **slice** it, it's going to be a **grate** time!

Carolyn Roddy

REASONS WHY

Print up a handout that folds in half. On the outside or front of the card print the words, "Good Reasons Why You Should NOT Attend (such and such meeting):"

When students open it, the inside is blank. Details of the meeting are printed on the back.
Dave Gallagher

ACTION HANDOUT

To advertise your youth meeting in a unique way, design a handout that folds in half, as illustrated. The front can be anything you want, as long as it is attractive and invites kids to open it and look inside. Inside print an assortment of puzzles, games, tongue twisters, and the like. On the back side of the handout, print all the details of your upcoming event. This not only gets your message across, but

gives kids a challenge as well. For added fun, supply answers to the puzzles at the meeting, and give prizes to anyone who answers all of them correctly.

CONTEMPORARY CARD HANDOUTS

Winning handouts not only gets the message across, but also contain a joke or humorous story to lead the reader into the advertising. One idea is to pattern them after contemporary greeting cards, but they don't have to be nearly that large. The front of the card carries the grabber line. Inside is the punch line or joke. The back side of the card can be used for the announcement.

After you write the copy, have someone draw the artwork. Then take the project to a quick print shop or create one on your computer and print it out yourself. A good size for this type of handout is half of a letter-sized sheet folded in half. That would make the front of the handout 5-by-4 inches.

To get you started, here are sample grabber lines with their punch lines.

- Grabber line: I taught my pet fish to sing for you, but lately he's been singing off-key...
    Punch line: ... and you know how hard it is to tuna fish.
        Tie-in: There's nothing fishy about...

- Grabber line: Latest clinical tests prove... seven out of 10 doctors...
    Punch line: ... Leaves three.
        Tie-in: Already proven...

- Grabber line: Choose your favorite nose: (pictures of noses)
    Punch line: Now... if you're done picking your nose...
        Tie-in: Blow on over to...

- Grabber line: Just so I wouldn't forget to tell you this, I tied my shoelace around my tongue.
    Punch line: Now I've got athlete's mouth.
        Tie-in: Don't Forget This!

- Grabber line: They say that success is 90 percent perspiration...
    Punch line: If that's so, you must be a tremendous success.
        Tie-in: A Program That's 100 percent Successful!

- Grabber line: The other day I saw a poor man who looked like he hadn't had a bite for weeks...
    Punch line: So I bit him.
        Tie-in: Put the bite on your friends to...

- Grabber line: I bought you two authentic pearl buttons from the South Sea Isle of Bali.
    Punch line: Now you'll be the only person in town with two Bali buttons.
        Tie-in: Isle meet you at...

- Grabber line: Beautify Junkyards!
    Punch line: Throw something lovely away today.
        Tie-in: A Beautiful Program!

- Grabber line: Stop! If you have any brains at all, you won't open this card!
    Punch line: Well, that settles that.
        Tie-in: Brains or no brains, come to...

- Grabber line: Get ready! Get set!
    Punch line: Get lost!
        Tie-in: Get on down to...

- Grabber line: Johnny, can you drive with one hand?
    Sure, baby!
    Punch line: Then wipe your nose; it's running.
        Tie-in: Drive on down to...

- Grabber line: Before you hang your clothes...
    Punch line: ... make sure they get a fair trial.
        Tie-in: Hung up? Meet the group at...

- Grabber line: Always cross the street with the light.
    Punch line: That is, if you can rip it out of the pavement.
        Tie-in: Rip on down to...

- Grabber line: How to Get Ahead
    Punch line: (picture of a guy chopping off some guy's head with an ax)
        Tie-in: You'll laugh your head off at...

- Grabber line: Note the sad story of the fleas.
    Punch line: They all go to the dogs.
        Tie-in: You can go to...

- Grabber line: This morning I got up, shaved, showered, and splashed a little toilet water on my cheeks . .
    Punch line: And then the lid fell and hit me on the back of the neck.
        Tie-in: Fall in at...

- Grabber line: My girlfriend is one of the twins.
    Really? How do you tell them apart?
    Punch line: Her brother wears glasses.
        Tie-in: An Unmistakable Program!

- Grabber line: How do you get down off an elephant?
    Punch line: You don't stupid, you get down off a duck!
        Tie-in: Head on down to...

- Grabber line: Open in Case of Fire
    Punch line: Not now, stupid! In case of FIRE!
        Tie-in: A Program That's Really Hot!

- Grabber line: Hey, why are you pulling that chain?
    Punch line: Did you ever try pushing one of these things?
        Tie-in: Push your friends to be at...

FREE TICKET

You can increase the likelihood of drawing a good crowd at a special event by printing up a free ticket. Use the ticket the same way you use a flier. Psychologically, the ticket has more drawing power than a flier or announcement. Even when you do not have an admission fee, a complimentary ticket gives people the feeling that they have something of value in their hands.

Use the one on page 70 or design your own. Simply include all the details of your event in the empty space either vertically or horizontally. You can hire a typesetter to typeset your information, create a ticket on your own computer, or have an artist letter it in an attractive way.

DIRECT MAIL

ADVELOPES

Every week or so you glance at the pile of old magazines in the corner of your office. You never use them, but you're loath to toss them because—well, you never know when they might come in handy.

Here's an immediate use for at least the colorful page ads—especially the ones in Christian

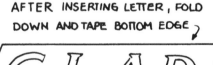

AFTER INSERTING LETTER, FOLD DOWN AND TAPE BOTTOM EDGE

FOLD UP AND TAPE EDGES

music magazines. Carefully cut them out and fold them into envelopes for mailing announcements for special activities. Group members will each get eye-grabbing, customized, one-of-a-kind envelopes.

Simply fold the ad twice, then tape the sides and later the flap. The address will probably get lost in the design unless you use a white self-adhesive label. *Len Cuthbert*

CODED MESSAGES

Need a new way to catch their attention? Find a computer program or font package that prints special symbols or other languages, and send coded messages to your kids.

In such a program, every letter on the keyboard corresponds to a character in the special font (see diagram). A message typed in usually looks like the English sentence you intended, but it prints out in the special symbols or characters. Make sure to include on the card where the kids can come to decipher the message—usually to your group meeting. Don't forget to bring the decoder sheet when you meet. *Greg Miller, Bob Mabry, and Paul Franceschini*

CALLING CARDS

Think up humorous or just plain weird business or organizational names to precede your return or forwarding address. The smiles you'll generate just might increase your readership. Try something like this:

Anointed Worm Ministries, Inc.
1217 S. Carrier Pkwy
Grand Prairie, TX 75051
"If God can use a worm, he can use you." See Jonah 4:7

COMPLIMENTARY TICKET

ADMIT
ONE

Put details of
your activity here

COMPLIMENTARY TICKET

ADMIT
ONE

Put details of
your activity here

COMPLIMENTARY TICKET

ADMIT
ONE

Put details of
your activity here

Here are some more examples:
• Elvis Is Alive International Headquarters (use this for your Elvis lovers)
• Mozart Is Alive International Headquarters (use this for your classical-music lovers)
Or, instead of being comical, you can add to the envelope an affirming touch:

Maker of Marvelous Melodies
Jill Reynolds
Box 111
Littleton, IN 68071

More examples of affirming address additions:
• Wonderful Grandparents
• Pat "The Patient" Pickleseed
• Harry "Helpful" Hines
• Gene "Gentle" Smith

Of course, avoid comments about a person's physical appearance, behavior, habits, family or cultural background (Mark "Meathead" Dormer) that are even close to derogatory, negative, or uncomplimentary comments. Nor should you flatter; be sure the statements are truthful and accurate. Choose only affirmations you can back up with reasons because the kids themselves may ask for evidence of the virtues you assign them. *Roger Haas*

Puzzle Piece Mailer

This little device is great for involving newcomers, making regulars feel special, and reaching out to inactives. The next time you plan a special party or event, buy a jigsaw puzzle and attach one piece to every invitation that you send. Explain how each person makes a unique contribution to the group and that each puzzle piece represents an individual.

Ask kids to bring their piece of the puzzle to the event to piece it together. Missing pieces—and people—will be noticed.

This idea encourages attendance by making kids feel welcome and giving them an important function at the beginning of the event. *Sylvan Knoblock*

Puzzling Publicity

Turn a drab publicity flier into an intellectual experience. Print a regular flier using lots of wording and a cartoon or drawing. Then cut each flyer into puzzle pieces. Mail one jumbled up flyer with an instruction sheet to each kid. Kids must put the puzzle together in order to read the announcement. *Christopher Snow*

Smile Postcards

One way to make your own mirror-image announcement cards is to type your message normally, make an overhead transparency of it, and then place the transparency in the photocopier so that it copies the message in reverse. *Rick Jenkins*

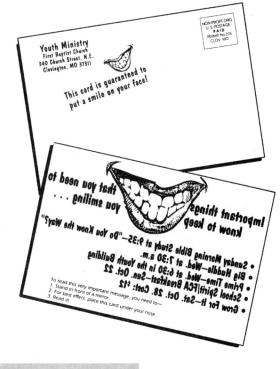

Letter From Afar

Teenagers are really impressed when they get a letter from a foreign country. Ask someone you know in another country to mail your kids letters announcing an upcoming event. Provide the person who does the mailing with addressed messages and money for postage.

This is an especially appropriate idea for a meeting with a missions emphasis. Missionaries could jot notes to your kids urging them to attend the meeting—or, better, yet, to come to their countries. If they receive a letter postmarked from somewhere like Zimbabwe or Honduras, it will really get their attention. *Frank Riley*

Air Mail

Want to remind kids of commitments they made at the last retreat? Of a big upcoming event? Look no further for an enthralling way to send quick notes to your kids. Inflate a light-colored balloon and tie it off with a paper clip or rubber band so that you can deflate it easily. With a fine-point, permanent-ink pen or marker (to prevent smudging), write your note on the balloon. You may want to use phrases like pumped up, air mail, lot of hot air, etc. Deflate the balloon and mail it in an envelope.

When your kids receive their balloon-notes, they'll either need a magnifying glass to read it—or have to blow it up. Chances are, they won't forget the message. *John Blackman*

FREE BROCHURES

Next time you're planning a big activity calendar for mailing to members of your group, contact the establishments you'll be patronizing in order to obtain their advertising brochures for free. Amusement parks, recreation areas, cities and towns, campgrounds, restaurants, and hotels often print up attractive, colorful fliers that you can add to your mailing to generate excitement and interest. *David Mahoney*

SCRAMBLED LETTER

Send your next flier in the form of a scrambled letter. First type your letter on a computer and number the lines. Make a copy of the letter that you can work with, but keep the original letter intact. Then scramble the order of the lines— with or without the numbers, depending on how challenging you want reading it to be. Include instructions and mail it off.

Why are you getting a scrambled letter? Because I know you can handle a challenge. Just read the lines of the letter in numbered order to find out what's next on our group's agenda.

Well, read on. Each line is numbered to show you which line to read next. Find line number 1 and go from there.

15 like us. Oh, and if you register early (by May 31), and attend all

2 that we do things in very unconventional ways in Junior High Vacation

5 ended up having fun. We do our own thing in our own room—even the

13 three-dimensional photo display for your room. It is real neat and

8 and play volleyball, and eat (donuts, pizza, and other yummies). Some-

1 You see, we have chosen this unusual letter to try to convince you

10 decide what). Of course, we have lessons too. That is the real meat

16 five days of VBS, you'll be eligible to win a portable CD player.

12 even keeps the church mice listening in. Our craft this year is a

14 you can personalize it if you want. Try us—we think that you'll

4 have attended Junior High VBS before. Some of the real grumps even

7 little kids. We even do our own music. Plus... we go on field trips

3 Bible School. If you don't believe us, just ask some of the kids who

9 times we bowl, play miniature golf, or go to a state park (you can help

11 of VBS but Mark is not your ordinary boring, preacher-type and he

6 missionary comes down to us instead of us sitting up with all the

Come join us,
 Mark Matthews
 Connie Flick
 Connie Hamilton

Connie Hamilton

THAT'S INCREDIBLE

List these, or other incredible facts, along with information on upcoming events the next time you print up a flier or reminder for your group. It could look something like this:

All of the following is absolutely, positively true!
- Wearing suspenders is illegal in Nogales, Arizona.
- Your statistical chance of being murdered is one in twenty thousand.
- Forty percent of American adults cannot fill out a bank deposit slip correctly.
- During his lifetime, the average American will eat 20,932 eggs and 4.1 tons of potatoes.
- The automatic transmission fluid in almost every car is whale oil.
- The average adult has enough iron in her body to make a two-inch nail.
- A Volkswagen has been compressed into a two-foot cube to serve as a coffee table for a Mahtomedi, Minnesota couple.
- Rats are fastidiously clean. "You dirty rat" slanders this furry pest. In addition, rats are not mentioned in the Bible.
- In Norton, Virginia, it's illegal to tickle a girl.
- TNT* will be at Lauren Butler's house this week, beginning at 7:01 sharp. Here's a map that's factually correct:

* Thursday Night Thing, where you get the facts of life... and more!

Len Woods

MAILER PRIZES

Do you wonder if your mailer gets read thoroughly? Try including a contest that requires kids to report important facts from the newsletter to you.

For example, print on your mailer that the person who is the fifteenth caller to a certain number after 3:30 p.m. on Monday, October 18 (any time and any date), wins a pizza, an album, concert tickets, or any other prize. Every caller must also answer several questions regarding upcoming activities announced in your newsletter. Many kids will read the entire newsletter to get the answers and make the call. The better the prize, the better your mailer will be read! *Todd Wagner*

MISSED-YOU LETTERS

Below are a batch of humorous letters to send when kids miss Sunday school or youth meetings. Be sure to keep track of who you send each letter to, so you don't send duplicates. And don't forget to write an occasional letter of appreciation to those who are always present. *Greg Thomas*

Dear Misser of the Marvelous Mysteries,

In view of the fact—whether or not a fact can be viewed is another matter entirely and shouldn't be allowed to confuse the issue. . . Of course, an issue must have some intelligence in order to become confused since any inanimate object or abstract concept is certainly not capable of thought and, therefore, it couldn't become confused. You should take great pleasure—I wonder if it's possible to take pleasure. Oh well, no matter—in knowing that you are not inanimate, since I am quite sure that by now you are thoroughly confused—that your presence was missing—a situation possibly only in conjunction with the absence of your person or body inasmuch as you are not a god and cannot have your presence present at any place where your person's presence or body's presence is not presently present—I felt compelled—or maybe it should be compulsed since the emotion that spawned this letter could more accurately be described as compulsion rather than compelsion. And please don't be alarmed that spawning usually has to do with fish giving birth; I have taken great liberties—is that possible?—already in this letter—to invite you to join us again this week.

See you,
    Greg

P.S. A prize awaits anyone who can correctly determine the message of this letter.

Dear fellow student of the hidden mysteries of God's eternally relevant and vitally dynamic message to mankind; in other words: Dear Student,

You probably didn't notice the mass exodus that took place last week—mainly because you weren't there to notice that you and several others weren't there.

Well, knowing that you are basically a conscientious person, I'm sure you've been punishing yourself severely for the tremendous anguish I have been experiencing due to your absence. Knowing also that you are basically kindhearted and unwilling to make a fuss, I suspect that you probably won't let me know the true reason for your absence.

I have, therefore, provided the following list of excuses, which sum up the five most likely reasons why a person would miss Sunday school. Simply check the appropriate box and hand it to me personally—folded, of course, so I won't know whose it is—this Sunday when you return to class.

☐ 1. The rug clashed with your outfit last time you came, and it was all you could do to keep from tearing your clothes off in order to avoid being such a spectacle.

☐ 2. Every time you think about coming to class the last time, a little voice in your head says, "The Devil made me do it."

☐ 3. Ever since we talked about angels several weeks ago, you've been scared stiff that God would give you your wings prematurely and let everybody know you are one.

☐ 4. Someone else put a dollar in the offering too, and you knew you couldn't afford two dollars the next week in order to gain your sense of superiority back.

☐ 5. You discovered that the blackboard was really green and you couldn't stand such hypocrisy in church.

Whatever the reason, we missed having you in class.

See you next Sunday,
    Greg

Dear Illustrious Imitator of Important Information,

I was inspired to institute an intensive investigation into an intriguing incident of infinite importance as a result of your insistence in being invisible in the institute of instruction—Sunday school.

Under such incredible inspiration I initiated this interesting interruption to your insidious and ill-advised invisibility hoping to intervene and incapacitate any increasing incidences of invisibility and incite you to intertwine with us this week at the institute of instruction.

I inestimably hope that this information is not inconsequential in impressing immediate interest to involve yourself invariably in our impressive and incomparable institute.

Inspirationally yours,
    Greg

Dear Succulent S_pper of the Savory Say_ngs,

_ have carefully co_posed a letter of _nf_n_te del_ght wh_ch _ know w_ll thr_ll and capt_vate you.

The object of th_s letter _s very s_ _ply to determ_ne wh_ch letters of the alphabet are _ _ss_ng fro_ th_s letter. Then you _ust arrange these letters alphabet_cally and say the_ three t_ _es _n qu_ck success_on.

Th_s w_ll enable you to answer the quest_on wh_ch _s the object of th_s letter. That quest_on _s: "Who _s _ _ss_ng fro_ Sunday school?" Say the letters now for the answer.

Now that you have establ_shed personal respons_b_l_ty for your act_ons, _ shall expect you to repent fully and to jo_n us aga_n th_s week.

See you,
    Greg Thomas

P.S. For another _nterest_ng exerc_se, try repeat_ng the follow_ng several t_ _es _n qu_ck success_on and see _f you can deter_ _ne the _ean_ng.
OWAH TAGU S_AM

Dear Resplendent Reveler in the Remarkable Revelation,

I recently reviewed the roster of registrants who regularly receive the remarkable revelations that recur without rarity each week at Sunday school.

Reevaluating the results, I realized that you resisted recognition last Sunday by removing the only real resource for recognition we retain: yourself. To help you resist a repetition of your recalcitrant and reprehensible recourse (which would realistically result in your rapacious ruination), I rallied my resources, rekindled my resolve, and wrote this ridiculous reading to reassure you that we missed you and really welcome your resolve to reappear without reluctance this week.

Rescusitatingly yours,
Greg

TRADEMARK LETTER

Use this idea to liven up regular youth group mailings. By going through magazines and catalogs, you can find lots of familiar trademarks to compose creative letters and announcements.

THIS IS A **GOODYEAR** FOR A BANQUET!

ANYONE CAN SURELY A **Ford** THIS AND I'M

NOT **LION**! INVITE **HOOVER** YOU'D LIKE TO, AND

IT WILL ONLY COST YOU **Penneys**. **SHELL** OUT

ONLY $4.50 PER PERSON AND YOU'LL BE HER

CHAMPION FOR PICKING UP THE **TAB**. OUR MUSIC

WILL BE **FOREMOST** IN THE FIELD. PUT YOUR

EXXON THE LINE & GET READY FOR A **SUPER**

TIME! **OK**? Jack

Just decide on your message and creatively work as many trademarks into it as possible. Glue them into position, write out your message, and make copies for distribution. The example shown here should give you the idea. *Jack Jones*

SACK MAIL

You can send paper lunch bags in the mail. Staple the open end shut, address the bag on one side, and print your message on the other side—or enclose it in the bag. Message ideas: "Get out of the sack next Sunday morning" or "This bag can be used to wrap fish—or to invite you to a rap session." Or "Blow this bag up and pop it—you'll get a bang out of our next event," etc. *Marjorie Walsleben*

WARNING ANNOUNCEMENT

Send a postcard one day with the following message: "Tomorrow you will receive a postcard. Read it." It is guaranteed that when you mail the second postcard the next day people will be anxiously waiting for it. *Patsy Quested*

PERSONALIZED PICTURE POSTCARDS

Here's an easy way to make personalized stationery, envelopes, or postcards. First get some magazines with nice photos in them. Magazines that are printed on heavier paper work best so that the ink doesn't show through on both sides. Colored pictures look best against the stark white of the paper you will be gluing them to.

Select a picture that you want to use. Use a little artistic judgment to pick out an interesting picture of the right size. Usually it is best to use one that is a little large, so that you can crop it to the size you want. Next, cut it out with an X-acto knife, or similar knife with a sharp, pointed blade. It's difficult to get a clean cut with scissors. Then glue it to the stationery, envelope, or card with glue (clear-drying, like rubber cement) or with spray adhesive (available in art stores). Wait for it to dry and carefully trim off the excess around the edge of the paper (see diagram). Neatness counts!

1. Cut out desired pictures with X-acto knife

2. Glue or spray mount back side. Remember, less is more.

3. Place it in position with lots of overlap. Let it dry.

4. Trim edge carefully. Wise precaution— make sure you leave room for a stamp and address if you plan to mail it

Since this whole process involves the use of sharp instruments, it is not recommended for small children or even unsupervised teens. But with a little care, patience, and thought, almost anyone can create one-of-a-kind stationery for themselves or for a gift. By the way, this is also a good way to use those old envelopes you have stashed away—you know, the ones with the out-of-date address on them. Just cover it with a nice picture! *Brian Buniak*

A Bagful of Great Mailers

Despite rising postage costs, the mail is still one of the best ways to announce upcoming events. Compile an up-to-date list of names and addresses that you mail to regularly. If you can keep enough names on your mailing list, you can mail bulk rate, to keep costs down.

The samples on pages 76-79 should get your creative juices flowing. Kids look forward to getting unusual and humorous letters in the mail. As long as you are taking the time to prepare a letter of some kind, it may as well be a good one. It usually costs no more to be creative.

Make your letters reader friendly with clip art and lettering. Rather than printing mailers on church letterhead (boring!), create your own group letterhead that includes your church name and address on it. Lots of colorful, unusual paper styles are available at stationery stores. Just take advantage of all the creative sources available to you.

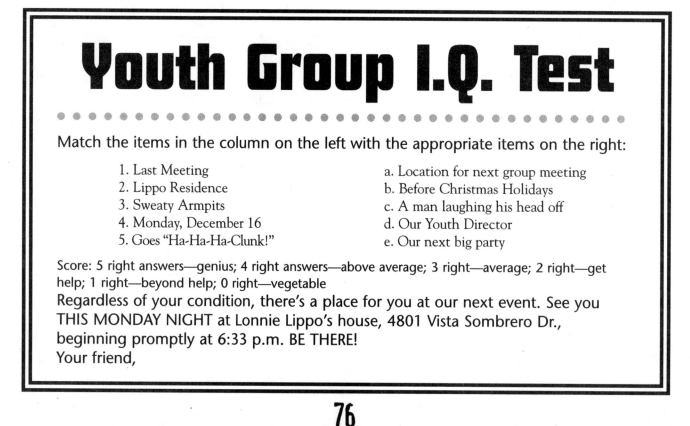

Youth Group I.Q. Test

Match the items in the column on the left with the appropriate items on the right:

1. Last Meeting
2. Lippo Residence
3. Sweaty Armpits
4. Monday, December 16
5. Goes "Ha-Ha-Ha-Clunk!"

a. Location for next group meeting
b. Before Christmas Holidays
c. A man laughing his head off
d. Our Youth Director
e. Our next big party

Score: 5 right answers—genius; 4 right answers—above average; 3 right—average; 2 right—get help; 1 right—beyond help; 0 right—vegetable

Regardless of your condition, there's a place for you at our next event. See you THIS MONDAY NIGHT at Lonnie Lippo's house, 4801 Vista Sombrero Dr., beginning promptly at 6:33 p.m. BE THERE!

Your friend,

If you thought our

LAST MEETING

was good, wait till you get a load of **this** one...

What Goes "Ho-Ho-Ho-Thud!"?

Answer: It's Santa Claus laughing his head off.

Yule laugh your head off at the next exciting _____, next Wednesday night at 6:30. Don't miss it!

Dear Student,
A routine check of school records has disclosed that you failed to complete kindergarten. We must, therefore, call to your attention Municipal Regulation 55-2938,11:

"KINDERGARTEN MUST BE COMPLETED BY EVERY RESIDENT OF THIS COMMUNITY. THIS MANDATORY REQUIREMENT FOR A RESIDENTIAL PERMIT CANNOT BE WAIVED UNDER ANY CIRCUMSTANCES."

Your lack of kindergarten certification causes us to hereby order you to report for kindergarten registration on the first WEDNESDAY before the new term begins. In view of your advanced age, however, it will not be necessary for you to bring along your mommy. Registration for the coming semester starts this **WEDNESDAY** night.

To Whom It May Concern:
   The Traffic Ticket Accounting Bureau wishes to inform you that its records indicate an overpayment on your part for traffic tickets.
   We cannot refund this overpayment, but you could do us a favor by hurriedly running up another traffic violation so that we may balance our books.
   Therefore, we strongly urge you to speed on over to the next exciting meeting of _____.

Congratulations!!!

   You are one of the lucky winners in our exciting WIN A BUCK contest!
   Your male deer will be sent to you under separate cover. If, however, you do not receive your buck by next Tuesday night, then bring this card to the special Winner's Meeting at Kathy Hoaky's house, Tuesday night at 7 sharp.

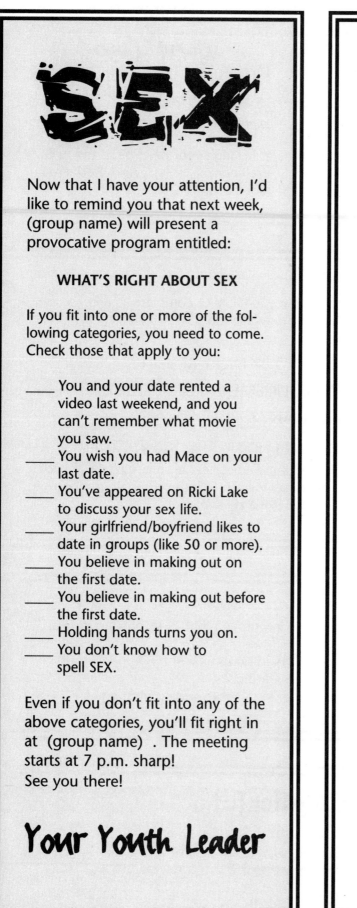

SEX

Now that I have your attention, I'd like to remind you that next week, (group name) will present a provocative program entitled:

WHAT'S RIGHT ABOUT SEX

If you fit into one or more of the following categories, you need to come. Check those that apply to you:

____ You and your date rented a video last weekend, and you can't remember what movie you saw.
____ You wish you had Mace on your last date.
____ You've appeared on Ricki Lake to discuss your sex life.
____ Your girlfriend/boyfriend likes to date in groups (like 50 or more).
____ You believe in making out on the first date.
____ You believe in making out before the first date.
____ Holding hands turns you on.
____ You don't know how to spell SEX.

Even if you don't fit into any of the above categories, you'll fit right in at (group name) . The meeting starts at 7 p.m. sharp!
See you there!

Your Youth Leader

The All-Purpose Letter

(Check one from each category:)

Dear:
____ Granny
____ Fingers
____ Elvin
____ Swinger

Just wanted to tell you that I have been:
____ watching my weight.
____ in love with my history teacher for the past two years.
____ picking my nose while thinking of you.
____ washing my socks.

After reading this letter, I hope you:
____ still feel like calling me Poopsie.
____ get paroled soon.
____ brush your teeth.
____ fall out the nearest three-story window.

Well, I have to close now because:
____ I don't know any more three-syllable words.
____ I need to study for my aerobics exam.
____ my mother is going to dress me.
____ my nose is bleeding.

Signed,
____ Sly Stallone
____ Mama Bear, Papa Bear & Baby Bear
____ Your mother
____ A Keebler elf

P.S. (event) next Sunday night, 6:30 at the church.

PARTY I.Q. TEST

● ●

Here is your personal copy of the Party IQ Test. It will determine how much fun you will be at a party and will indicate the areas in which you need to improve. Answer the following questions true or false (circle your answer):

• Kissing is when you grab another person's right hand with your right hand and shake it vigorously.
True/False.

• The best way to behave at a party is to prop against a wall, with one foot against the wallpaper, looking cool.
True/False.

• The most accepted way of getting more salsa for your chips is to dip your hand into the sauce while joking, "Well, we all have the same germs anyway."
True/False.

• The proper time to leave the party is at 3:00 in the morning or when the host's family comes downstairs for breakfast.
True/False.

To check your answers, bring this test to the next (event), which just happens to be this Thursday night at 7:00. We may wind up having a party of our own! Don't miss it!

This Postcard Entitles You to One Free Night in County Jail.
(Tax and tip extra)

In order to receive this valuable free offer, merely follow the steps listed below:

1. Write down the important address below and keep it.
2. Crumple this card into a little ball.
3. Cram it down the throat of the nearest police officer.

This postcard is also good for one great evening at (youth event) in case you decide not to take advantage of the free offer above. Meet us at Bob Frit's house, 4040 Yucko Street, at exactly 7:13 p.m. See ya there.

You May Have Already Won a Valuable Prize!!!

Here is your lucky number: **37586**

If the lucky number above matches the winning number below, which was drawn at random (of course), then you may have won all or none of these exciting prizes:

• An all-expenses-paid trip for two to Temecula (one way).
• An autographed picture of Elmer Floggy.
• Three tickets to the Museum of Antique Lawn Mowers.
• One pound of minced raccoon livers.

Here is the winning number: **37586**

If your lucky number matches the winning number you may, or may not, have won the lovely prizes listed above. For further instructions, bring this card to (youth event) this Wednesday night, 7:00 at the church.

STRIKE THREE, YOU'RE OUT

On page 81 are four absentee letters you can send to teens on their first, second, third, and fourth absences. It's a lighthearted way to let your students know you're concerned and miss them. Mail them out in the order shown here—you'll probably get a good response. Change the copy on each letter to fit your own group. *Jim Walton*

BULLETIN BOARDS

THE BIG PICTURE

Create a floor-to-ceiling notepad using four-by-eight-foot sheets of white bathroom paneling. Dry eraser markers work well on these boards. They make a great billboards for serious message—prayer lists, announcements—or canvases for creative doodlers. *Tim Stoica*

TABLETOP PUBLICITY BOARDS

Short of bulletin board space? No bulletin boards period? Lean one or two six- or eight-foot folding tables up against the wall. You can tape announcements or whatever to the tabletops avoiding the damage that tape does to most walls. Add streamers, balloons, etc., to a creatively arranged couple or three tables. And with a little muscle power, these publicity boards are even portable. *Russ Porter*

PHOTO ENDORSEMENTS

Do you routinely photograph your students at various get-togethers? If you don't, start the habit now. When you accumulate an inventory of photos, use them for publicity purposes this way: When you need to publicize an event, select and mount photos of teens in your group.

Next think up entertaining and informative dialogue about the upcoming events to place inside comic strip-style dialogue bubbles attributed to the teens in the photos. Make them fun without embarrassing anyone. If you feel the pho-

tos might be torn down, mount them inside a large glass poster frame.

Your kids will watch for these from week to week. *Bill Swedberg*

FIFTY REASONS TO BELONG TO A YOUTH GROUP

Add an occasional cartoon to the list on page 82, and use it as a handout, a mailer, or on a bulletin board.

Carol Eklund

BULLETIN BOARD TREE

If bulletin board space is at a premium, build a bulletin board tree for hanging several announcements at a time. If it's portable, you can cart it around to

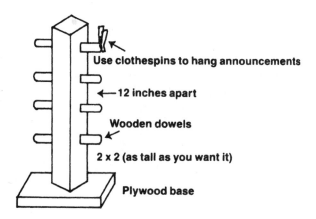

Use clothespins to hang announcements

← 12 inches apart

Wooden dowels

2 x 2 (as tall as you want it)

Plywood base

all your group functions. Hang up a few humorous things on occasion—cartoons, crazy pictures, etc.—and kids will look forward to checking it out whenever they see it. *David Washburn*

PLAN AHEAD

If your group takes an annual excursion to an amusement park, recreational area, or camp, be sure to think about next year's publicity on this year's trip. Take a camera and snap photos or shoot video of the group members riding, eating, laughing, talking, singing, giggling, or clowning.

The next time you need to promote the event, show edited versions of the video from the last event as commercials. Also use the photos to make posters and bulletin board displays. *Dan Craig*

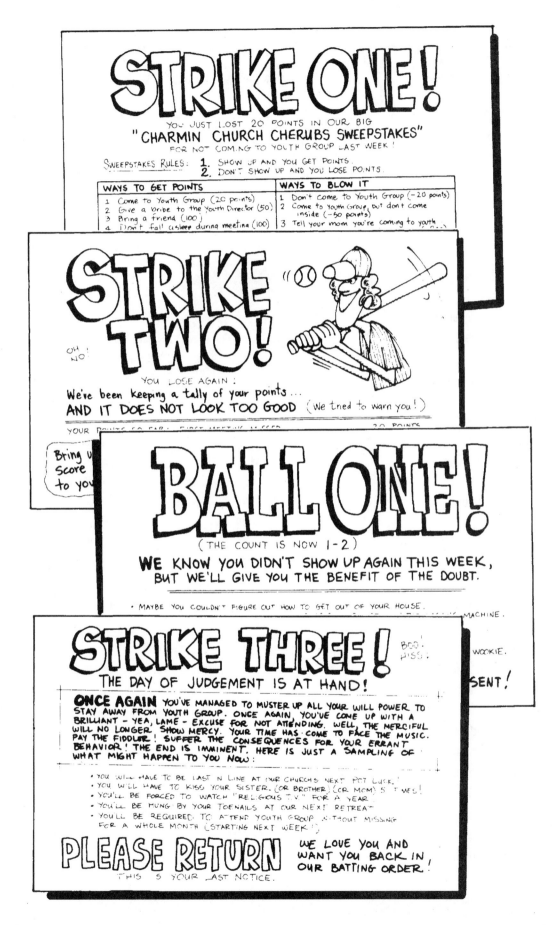

Fifty Reasons to Belong to a Youth Group

1. To study the Bible.
2. To be with friends.
3. Rutabagas will absolutely never be served for refreshments.
4. It's nonfattening.
5. It could prevent flat feet.
6. To have fun.
7. You don't have to wear water wings to participate.
8. It's better than doing homework.
9. It isn't at 5 a.m.
10. To grow in your faith.
11. There are no finals.
12. You may win valuable prizes.
13. Brussels sprouts will never be served as refreshments.
14. To meet new friends.
15. To play silly games.
16. We need you.
17. The leaders care about you.
18. It is almost never fatal.
19. There are no homework assignments.
20. For support.
21. Ten out of ten doctors recommend it.
22. To help plan things that you want to do.
23. It has the Good Housekeeping Seal of Approval.
24. Like Mount Everest, it is there.
25. It is a known cure for the midweek blahs.
26. (For girls) Guys are there.
27. (For guys) Girls are there.
28. It doesn't cause bad breath.
29. To be with other Christians.
30. It's free.
31. For fellowship.
32. It contains absolutely no cholesterol.
33. Bert and Ernie think it's great.
34. There are people who want to liste to you.
35. Your youth leaders will do all your homework for you. (Just kidding.)
36. "Seinfeld" and "Friends" aren't on Wednesday nights.
37. To share ideas.
38. No previous experience is required.
39. You will get mail.
40. You will have lots of dates. (We'll send you a calendar.)
41. You will like it.
42. To learn more about God.
43. We give double coupons.
44. You are important.
45. There has never been a major earthquake in the youth room.
46. While it contains no fluoride, it has never caused a cavity.
47. To come and pray together.
48. To get to know each other.
49. It is not lite.
50. After you have taken time to read all 50 of these reasons, you may as well give it a try. See you at youth group on _____!

SCHIZOPHRENIC PORTRAITS

Take everyone's picture; use a plain background and make sure each subject is the same distance from the camera and centered—not off to the right or left—looking straight forward. Cut each picture in half, right under the eyes, straight across. Then match every person's top half to someone else's bottom half and mount on the stiff paper that comes with the film. Hang the finished photos on your youth bulletin board. They'll be quite an attraction. *Kathryn Lindskoog*

CANDID PHOTOS

If you have trouble getting kids to read the news and announcements hung on the youth group bulletin board, try this. Have someone shoot candid photos of all your youth activities and each week hang a new batch of pictures on the board. Kids love to see themselves and others in action, and they'll make it a point to check out the bulletin board every week. Appropriate humorous captions can be placed under each photo for added fun. *Ray Peterson*

PEEP BOX

This simple idea is a great way to get kids to read bulletin board information. Build a big box out of plywood. The box should be about three feet wide by three feet deep by three feet high. Mount it on legs and cut a hole in the bottom of the box just big enough for a kid to stick his head through. Paint the outside of the box or decorate it in some creative way.

One side of the box should be hinged so that it can open up and then be locked shut. A small light bulb of some kind inside the box—battery operated, perhaps—will light up the inside of the box. On the inside of the four walls of the box, hang your posters, announcements, pictures, and other items of interest. Kids now have to get under the box and poke their heads up through the hole in the bottom in order to see what is inside the box. If you are creative, and change the contents of the box every week, kids will stand in line to see what is inside, just to satisfy their curiosity. Those same kids might ignore a traditional bulletin board.

A variation on this is to blacklight the inside the box and do all of your signs and announcements with fluorescent or glow-in-the-dark markers or paints. The effect is fascinating.

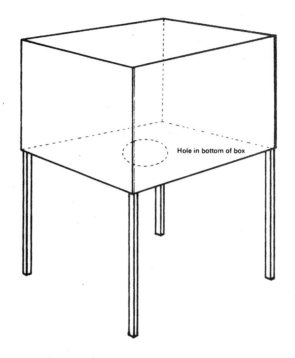

Hole in bottom of box

To get the best use out of your peep box, place it in a strategic location where lots of kids pass by (such as a popular youth hangout or on a school campus—you'll need permission—or near the school). *Paul Sailhamer*

BOX BULLETIN BOARD

Make boxes with a small hole in one end (to see into the box) and a slit on top of the box for light. Place announcements, photos, etc., on the inside of the box opposite the peek hole. Attach the boxes at eye level on the youth bulletin board. The novelty of the boxes will attract many who would ordinarily ignore the bulletin board.

CREATIVE GUNNY SACKS

With the use of burlap bags, you can make interesting and attractive murals, bulletin boards, or framed pictures. All you do is mount and paint on them with oil paint or thick poster paint—or use magic markers. The results can be very effective. *Bobby Shows*

POSTERS

SURPRISE PHOTOS

Kids love seeing themselves in photos. Collect posters and cardboard displays from movies or TV programs. Snap photos of youth group members and tape their faces over the faces of the stars.

For example, a poster from a popular television show pictures seven kids in a beach scene. Substitute five faces from your youth group and leave two original faces on each end. Announce youth group events and activities on the corners of the posters. *Valerie Hobbie*

COLOR POSTERS

Tired of plain old black and white? A little work on your part turns your copy machine into a color copier.

Create a clip-art poster or similar artwork to a point that it can be photocopied cleanly. If you plan to color your letters, they will have to be outline style. Solid letters will be black no matter what.

Copy the poster onto several different colored sheets—construction paper will work on a machine with a hand feeder. Use one copy of whichever color you wish your background to be as the master poster.

Cut out parts of the subjects from the different colored copies, and glue them in place on the master

poster. For example, cut a person's hair out of brown paper, pieces of clothing out of red, and so on.

If you plan to display permanent posters as door signs, etc., you may wish to seal them in plastic covers. *Len Cuthbert*

TITANIC ADVERTISING

Want to make a quality banner or huge poster but feel you can't draw? Using clip art, rub-on letters, or your computer, create your poster on unlined, white, letter-sized paper. Then use a photocopier to transfer your creation to an overhead transparency.

Place the sheet on an overhead projector and focus the image onto butcher paper taped to a large wall. (You can even have your artwork cover an entire wall.) Outline the images using black water paint and a medium-sized brush that allows you to keep detail. When the outline is complete, turn off the projector and fill in the giant letters and figures with water paints of whatever colors suit your design. The process works as well for creating theatrical backdrops. *Len Cuthbert and Dan Pryor*

LOCKER POSTERS

A favorite pastime of many junior high and high school students is decorating the insides of their lockers. They plaster them with pictures, pins, stickers, license plates, concert posters, tickets, and the like.

You can use this to your advantage by designing creative locker posters, tailored especially for the inside of a locker door. Get the measurements from your local campus (the average high school locker door is 12 inches wide) and design a poster that your kids will be proud to display. It can promote the youth group or be just a positive poster that helps kids to share their faith with friends. *Robert Crosby*

84

SHRINKING POSTER

Want to keep your teenagers' parents informed of upcoming activities, especially those that require parental permission? Print up a poster with announcements and details on the front and parental permission forms on the back that are positioned back-to-back with the corresponding announcements on the front.

Have group members take their posters home and hang them up in their rooms. When an activity takes place, a young person clips the section from the poster for that activity, asks a parent to fill out the form on the back, and turns it in. As time passes, the poster grows smaller as each activity is clipped. *Cinda Warner Gorman*

CELEBRITY ANNOUNCEMENTS

How would you like to have Sandra Bullock, Tom Cruise, or Steve Martin endorse one of your youth group activities?

Here's how to set it up. Contact either a local movie theater or video store and ask the manager if you can have the life-size posters that they use to advertise hit movies. They're usually thrown away after the advertising campaign is over.

Then convert the poster into an ad for one of your events. For example, have a life-sized Tom Cruise say, "I'm going to camp this summer. See you there." The kids will love it. *Joey Potter*

BILLBOARD POSTERS

Poster-making can be both fun and useful, especially if the poster you are making is billboard size. If you explain your purpose to an outdoor advertising company, they will usually be happy to give you old billboard posters free. These posters come in sheets of heavy paper about five by eight feet and are great for making giant posters. Provide plenty of floor space, big paint brushes, and water-base paint and let your kids get as creative as they want. *Calvin Pearson*

SILK-SCREEN PRINTING

Or How to Produce Good-looking, Professional Posters at a Good-looking, Nonprofessional Price.

The days of slopped-together posters are over. No longer will something made from magazine clippings, rubber cement, water paint, and markers with a generous helping of glitter be read, let alone get any response. When you want to create something other than computer-generated ads, try silk-screening. Anybody can create silk screens. That includes you!

The silk-screen process is a unique form of stencil printing that enables you to print on just about any surface in nearly any color, size, or quantity. We are going to explain step-by-step how to build your own silk screen and how to operate it. The costs are surprisingly low, and the procedure is amazingly simple.

• The Silk Screen Itself

A silk screen consists of a wooden frame with silk attached to it and stretched out. The frame is attached with hinges to a flat piece of plywood. You can purchase it ready-made or build one yourself, which is the most economical.

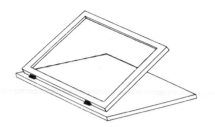

• How To Build a Silk-Screen Frame

The frame is simply four pieces of wood, fastened into a rectangular shape. The wooden pieces should be approximately 1_-by-1_ inches in size. It is best to miter the joints at a 45-degree angle, and nail with any nail of reasonable length. For added strength, use four metal "L" braces at the joints.

After you determine what poster size you will use most often, make sure that the inner dimensions of the frame are at least three inches larger all around than the dimensions of the poster size.

• The Silk

You will need to buy silk (12xx pure screening silk) a little larger than your frame. It runs about seven dollars a yard, and comes a yard wide. Usually a half yard will cover most poster screens no larger than 18 inches wide. The silk is stretched tightly across the frame, and stapled. There are other methods of attaching the silk, but the stapling method is the simplest and easiest for the beginner. Start at one corner and work around, pulling the silk tight, and stapling at one-inch intervals. Staple on an angle for the most effective hold. For best results, wet the silk first with warm water, and leave it wet while stretching it; then dry it later. After the silk is attached, trim off excess silk.

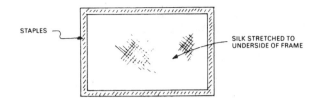

After it is stapled, smear some white glue over the staples and let dry. This will prevent future tearing loose of the silk.

• Hinge Frame To a Flat Surface

Buy a small pair of hinges with removable pins. Also you will need a piece of plywood (_-to-_ inches thick will do) to serve as a base. Plywood dimensions should be a little larger than the outside dimensions of the frame.

• The Stencil

Now you are ready to print some posters. You need a basic design for a poster first; this can be drawn with a pencil or copied from another picture and adapted for your own use. Anybody who can trace can make a stencil.

To make a stencil, the basic pattern (your own poster idea) is cut out of a film called Knife-cut Lacquer film, which can be purchased from an art store or from a silk-screen supply house. It consists of a shiny, soft amber-colored film affixed to a dull plastic backing sheet.

Tape down your original design to a flat surface (desktop, etc.). You will need plenty of light. Work in a comfortable position. Cut a piece of lacquer stencil film just big enough to cover your design. Tape this film in position over the design, shiny side up.

Next, you will need an X-acto knife with a #11 blade. This can be bought at any art store.

Keep the blade sharp. Dull blades only cause trouble. Make a test cut. In a corner of the film, cut a small triangle. CUT THROUGH THE SHINY LACQUER FILM ONLY! DO NOT CUT THROUGH THE BACKING SHEET! Insert the blade of your knife under the film in one corner of the triangle. Lift the film and strip away the triangle of lacquer film (for practice).

Follow this procedure over your whole pattern—trace, cut, strip away the lacquer film—until you have removed film from all areas indicated on your pattern. The stripped or open areas will be those through which your ink will be impressed onto the printing surface. Remember, do not cut through or into that backing sheet. It is there to hold the stencil together. Always keep the film smooth and flat. Do not crease it.

Place the completed stencil between the silk—attached to the frame, of course—and the plywood surface, positioned in the center of the frame. It's a good idea to put the stencil on top of a few sheets of your stock (the paper you are printing on) to give the stencil a little added height. Then, lower the screen (frame and silk) onto the stencil. The stock under the stencil acts to bring the stencil sheet and silk into good contact. The stencil and silk must be in contact at all points in order to adhere well.

• Attach the Stencil

Now you are ready for the adhering process. You need two small, soft rags. Wet one rag with some adhering solvent or a good quality lacquer thinner. Either works fine, except that a special adhering solvent is usually more potent. The rag should be damp, but not dripping wet. With this rag you rub (from the top side) the silk where the stencil shows through. Rub one area at a time, using firm strokes, and you will see the film actually adhere. It sort of changes color. Immediately after using the wet rag, rub the same area with a dry rag to soak up any excess adhering liquid. Too much liquid burns or actually begins to dissolve the film. Follow each series of wetting strokes with drying strokes of the drying rag. Make sure the stencil adheres evenly all over. The stencil is now adhered to the silk.

Let it dry for about 15 minutes. Then raise the screen and pull off the backing sheet. Pull down a corner of this backing sheet and slowly and carefully peel off until the entire sheet is removed. Caution: Always perform the adhering process in a warm, dry atmosphere.

• Set the Register Guides

Put a piece of stock under the stencil (now adhered to the silk) and adjust to the position in which the pattern is centered, straight, etc. You will want to put some register guides or edge guides along two edges of the stock, so that all printing will print in the same place on every sheet. This is especially important for multicolored printing.

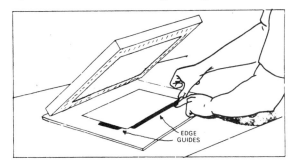

The edge guides can be made from pieces of thin cardboard or from pieces of masking tape. Anything that will stay in place will work.

• Block Out

Now you need to block out all open areas of the silk around the edges of the stencil. This can be done many ways, but one good way is to cover the area on the underside of the silk with masking tape. When this is done, you are ready to begin printing. The idea of blocking out is to leave open only the image that you want printed so that ink can pass through.

OPEN SILK AREA ("BLOCK-OUT" THIS AREA WITH TAPE.)

LACQUER FILM (STENCIL) DO NOT BLOCK OUT THIS AREA

• Print

To print, you need to buy a squeegee, a piece of wood with a strip of a specially treated rubber attached to it.

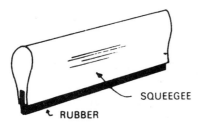

SQUEEGEE

RUBBER

This can be purchased at a good art store or a silk-screen supply house. The squeegee should be about one-half inch shorter than the smallest inside dimension of your frame.

Put one piece of paper in the edge guides. Lower the screen onto it. Pour some silk-screen ink (regular paint will not work) at one end of the screen on top of the silk. With the squeegee, you pull the ink firmly across the pattern—once or twice at the most—and then lift the screen up. The paper will probably stick to the underside of the screen which is okay. Pull it off and look at it. You have just silk-screened! Lay the printed stock somewhere to dry and keep going. You can print as many copies as you want. If you are getting unwanted ink on your paper, chances are you need to block out areas you missed with tape.

• Clean Up

The screen must be cleaned after every operation. If you want to save the stencil and use it again, then you must leave it attached to the silk. Once you take it off, it is gone. So if you want to use it again, merely clean off all the masking tape and wash the ink off with paint thinner. (Do not use lacquer thinner.) Use plenty of rags and get the ink completely off. You can use the stencil over and over again. To take the stencil off, leaving the silk ready for the next stencil, simply soak it off with lacquer thinner—or adhering solvent, which is

more expensive. When the silk is clean, you can attach a new stencil at any time in the future.

• Items to Purchase

Frame and plywood back
Silk
Squeegee
Stencil film
X-acto knife
Masking tape 191
Lacquer thinner (or adhering solvent)
Paint thinner
Silk-screen ink
Paint rags and a putty knife

Most well-stocked art stores carry a line of silk-screen supplies. Check the Yellow Pages of your phone book for a dealer or call a sign shop and ask where they get their supplies.

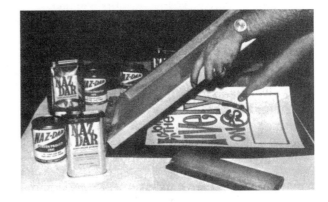

ASK SOMEONE WHO KNOWS

The following is the one-and-only, all-purpose poster idea. No matter what you want to advertise, this poster will do it. It needs no specific information whatsoever. The poster simply reads "Ask Someone Who Knows."

If you wish to advertise on a school campus, for example, the poster can by hung at various places all over the school, and the kids from your youth group can wear a little sticker reading "I Know."

The principle is fairly simple: Kids around school see a sign that tells them to ask someone "who knows," so they ask your kids who are wearing the "I know" stickers. Of course your kids can then unload all the information about your next meeting or special event and also give the person who asked an "I know" sticker, because now he knows too! This subtle but effective means of advertising will also work in a school that does not allow religious or church posters on campus. The poster really says nothing to offend anybody. Matching posters and stickers are easily silk screened.

LESSON RECOLLECTION

Most individuals—especially junior highers—retain even the single main point of a sermon or lesson only with difficulty.

To overcome this obstacle to learning, try this idea. During a long series of lessons, set a sheet of poster board in the room. Each week bring an object that symbolizes the main point of the lesson—a salt packet from a fast-food restaurant for a lesson from Matthew 5 ("You are the salt of the earth"), a 100-dollar bill of Monopoly money for a lesson from 2 Corinthians 9 ("Each man should give what he has decided in his heart to give, not reluctantly or under compulsion, for God loves a cheerful giver"), etc.

At the conclusion of the lesson, the object is attached to the growing collage of knickknacks

that are miscellaneous to anyone but your students—for at the beginning of each week's lesson, they're sure to associate the posted objects with the corresponding lessons. Soon they may want to feel some ownership of the board by adding their own magazine clippings and such.

The visual continuity of a lesson-recall board can give a group a sense of history and belonging, too. *Mary Gillett*

WANTED POSTER

Wanted posters printed with space available for a cartoon characterization or a humorous photograph evoke great results because of the personal attention they afford. For someone in your group with artistic ability, this can be a good weekly project.

When a person does something funny, post his boo-boo on the bulletin board. Mail them to youth program absentees, filling in a ridiculous name, such as "Ding-a-ling DeeDee" or "Insane Duane." Then write in what they are wanted for, such as Sunday school, youth choir, etc. *Bryant Wilson*

POSTER CONTEST

Give each team a stack of magazines, magic markers, poster paints, poster board, rubber cement, etc., and from these materials, each team is to make posters describing some special event. Winning posters are chosen for originality, humor, etc., and appropriate prizes are awarded. This is a good way to get kids involved in advertising of your program. *Jerry Summers, Corpus Christi, Tex.*

PROMOTIONAL EVENTS

CALL IN AND WIN!

Getting kids to read and take note of a monthly calendar can be challenging. Add a little incentive. On the calendar days, sandwiched between event announcements, offer prizes with notes like this:
BE CALLER 3 AND WIN A FREE PIZZA!

The teen who calls the church on that date and is the right number caller wins. Ideally, list the phone number of an answering machine (not your church secretary) so you can cope with what may be a flood of calls into your office. But at least they'll be reading about upcoming events and activities they might otherwise miss! *Tim Greilich*

YOUTH CALLING CARDS

As a visual reminder of who's missing, make up index cards for every youth involved in your program, complete with addresses, phone numbers, and any other helpful information (school activities, work location, and so on). Make up cards for youth prospects also.

Print each teen's name in large letters at the top or on the back of the index card, and then tack all of the cards to a bulletin board, using push pins. Label this board "Missing in Action," and mount it on the wall or the door of the meeting room. Consider making multiple copies of the cards in case some are lost.

Instruct the youths who attend the meetings to transfer their own cards to an adjacent bulletin board labeled "Here and Now." Then it should be easy to

see who's missing from meetings. At the end of the meeting, ask kids and youth leaders to take the Missing in Action cards as a reminder to call or send a note to the missing students. They must return the card at the next meeting. Ask people not to take the same missing person's card two weeks in a row.

Before the next meeting, return the Here and Now cards to the Missing in Action board so that you're ready to use them again. *Greg Miller*

WELCOME POSTCARDS

Inundate incoming kids with welcoming mail around promotion time.
1. Shortly before promotion, scan the Sunday school lists for names and addresses of youths graduating into your group.
2. Ask for volunteers (whatever number is practical) from your youth group to address postcards. Each new member's name and address should show up on 30 cards.
3. While the group is addressing postcards, brainstorm 30 topics relating to the youth group—activities, studies, food, games, service projects, singing, etc.
4. Assign each volunteer one of the topics, and give that volunteer one set of preaddressed cards. If there are 14 incoming youths, for instance, each volunteer receives one card addressed to each of the 14—or 14 cards total. The volunteers then write a brief note to each new kid about an assigned topic. Veteran members can assist newer members with necessary information. All cards must be turned in to the church office within the week.
5. About a week before the incoming kids start attending youth group, begin a daily mail campaign using the prewritten postcards. Stamp and mail a topical set of cards every day for 30 straight mailing days. New members who receive daily postcards from peers attend their first meeting with excitement and enthusiasm. *Jeff Elliott*

ROUNDBALL ROUND-UP

Meet your kids at church on a Saturday afternoon, and bring as many basketballs as possible. Divide into teams and disperse around town. Have teams go to schools, apartment complexes, parks—wherever there are hoops—and begin playing basketball. As other teens and children pass by, invite them to join the game. Introduce yourselves, get to know the kids, and invite them to church. *John Peters*

Booster Placards

Here's a good way to build a positive image for your youth group on campus—and build school spirit at the same time. Print up booster placards, 11 by 14 inches or so, with a "Go Team!" slogan on one side, and on the other side general information—like the team roster, the team schedule, an announcement for your youth group, etc.

Print the placards on heavy card stock and in the school's colors. Get permission from school officials ahead of time; then have your kids distribute them to all the rooters in the stands.

You may want to print something humorous on the back of the placard, like this:

Suggested placard uses:
• Raise it and holler to show your support for your team.
• Form a card section with others who also have them.
• Use it as a collar-shaper for your shirts instead of starch.
• Use it to line your cat's litter box.
• Use it as an umbrella if it rains.

Video Awards

Create a nonthreatening way for kids not only to invite their friends to events, but to prove that the activities are actually fun. For every event, recruit a volunteer video photographer to tape the highlights. Kick off the activities by announcing that the most enthusiastic participant of the evening will receive an award at the end of the event. Give the winner a certificate or button as well as the videotape of the night's events. *Len Cuthbert*

Sponsor Sweepstakes

In a day of ten-million-dollar sweepstakes, methods of recruiting sponsors for retreats, camps, and lock-ins may need an update. *Tom Daniel*

GROCERY BAG PROMOTION

This idea combines public service with advertising aimed at the general public—for upcoming church events. See if a local supermarket will allow your youth group to work for a day bagging groceries for customers and carrying their groceries out to the car—for free. Make sure the kids who do the bagging get instructions on how not to crush food items.

Into each bag of groceries drop a flier advertising a church event (car wash, spaghetti dinner, canned food drive, etc.), or staple the flier onto the bag. It's a good image-builder and a great way to advertise. *David Washburn*

CATERPILLAR EATING CONTEST

Make some posters and mail an advertisement of an upcoming eating contest. The delicacy will be...caterpillars! Be sure to include a note like this one: "We provide the caterpillars!" The kids will anticipate a relatively gross activity.

You won't be supplying your teens with real caterpillars. Instead you can make them individually or in a long trough. Here's the recipe:

Split a banana lengthwise and place it flat-side-down on a plate. Spray whipped cream in long lines down the back and sides. Decorate with green sprinkles and chocolate syrup stripes. Use pretzel sticks to make feelers, two cherry halves for eyes, and rows of raisins for feet.

The contest can be based on speed-eating, eating without hands, blindfold feeding, or team consumption. Kids will love it. *Jim Larsen*

YOUTH ARREST

Here's a way to familiarize the adults and the uninvolved youth in your church with the youth group. Have several of your young people or adult leaders dress up like police officers in rented costumes (some costume shops have a selection of contemporary police uniforms, Keystone Cops uniforms, or British bobby uniforms).

Have enough uniforms so that each entrance to the church can be manned by two "officers." You might want to hook up a traffic light in front of the church entrance or park a motorcycle by the door.

As teenagers enter the church, tell them that they are under arrest for being in violation of being a high school student. Take them aside and give them a written summons to appear before Youth Court the night of your youth meeting. When families without young people enter, briefly explain what you are doing and tell them about your youth group.

This is what the summons can say:

Certificate of Summons

You, _____ , are hereby and forthwith placed under arrest for being in _____ grade. Your arrest is made possible because of the long arm of the law handed down in the decision of The Supreme Judge in his very historic case in John, Chapter 3, Verse 16.

You are hereby and forthwith summoned to appear in court before de youth minister (Judge Wash) on September 21 in the basement of the Nativity School Courthouse. People's Court will start at 7:00 p.m. SHARP, where you shall be given a three minute trial. (Since de judge is known as "hang 'em high Washburn," your trial will be very short!) You will be sentenced to eat pizza and laugh a lot...but...not before working on Wash's chain gang for about an hour in a trade-in scavenger hunt.

If you wish to plead your case, you are free to bring a teenage lawyer friend who did not appear at church today.

Signed,
Dave Washburn
Senior Officer
and
Junior Officers:(kids' signatures)

David Washburn

TELEPHONE BLITZ

This idea is far from new, but it works. It is simply a plan to get the word out to as many kids as possible.

• **Step 1:** Begin collecting names and phone numbers of as many kids as possible. Old kids, new kids, anyone who is eligible to attend your meetings.

• **Step 2:** Appoint or elect a telephone chairman who is a real go-getter and can motivate people. This teen is in charge of every telephone blitz.

• **Step 3:** The telephone chairman enlists the help of a number of callers who will call up 10 people the evening before the meeting you want to advertise. (If you have a list of 100 people to call, you need 10 callers.) Each caller is given a list of 10 by the chairmen.

• **Step 4:** On the day of the telephone blitz (usually the day before the meeting), the telephone chairman contacts the callers to remind them to call up their 10 people to invite to the meeting tomorrow. Each caller should know all the details of the meeting, such as time, place, what the program will be, and so on. If the person called says he would like to come but doesn't have a ride, the caller tells him to be ready between say 7:00 and 7:30 (depending on when the meeting is) and someone will come by and pick him up. Each caller should be well-prepared for any question.

• **Step 5:** After the callers contact all 10 of their people, they report back to the chairman how many are coming, not coming, not reachable, need rides, etc.

• **Step 6:** The telephone chairman then calls a transportation chairman who has lined up cars available to pick up people. She informs the transportation chairman about whom to pick up, where they live, etc.

• **Step 7:** The transportation chairman calls the drivers of the available cars and assigns them people to pick up.

Below is a diagram of the procedure:

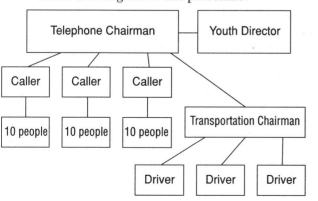

This procedure can be repeated over and over every week before your youth group meeting. This gets everybody involved and is extremely effective when carried out properly.

HAVE PHONE DIRECTORY, WILL TRAVEL

Promote group organization and interaction with a "shrink-wrapped" phone directory. Reduce your current youth group phone directory to a 2-x4-inch rectangle. Print eight to a sheet on card stock and have the sheet laminated at a copy shop. You'll save money if you cut the sheet apart yourself after lamination.

The resulting cards fit into a wallet, pocket, purse, on a key chain, in an organizer—and they're waterproof. They'll survive a shove into the pool and even a spin cycle. *Gene Stabe*

PARADE PANTOMIME

This idea work bests in smaller towns. It's an effective promotional event or just plain fun for your group. Contact a local radio station and ask it to play about 15 minutes of John Philip Sousa marches at a given time on a specific Saturday afternoon. If they agree to do that for you, you're in business.

Obtain a parade permit (if necessary) and have your kids form a marching band. Make or borrow uniforms or band costumes if possible. Also have every kid bring or borrow a portable boom box, not an instrument. At the appointed time, kids march down Main Street with their radios tuned to the radio station that agreed to play the band music. Crank up the sound. The marching band may look ridiculous but it sounds great. If it's advertised in advance, it will attract lots of attention. You may want to prepare some of your kids or leaders to talk with people along the parade route. Encourage them to invite kids to the youth group and adults to church services. Hand out flyers or tracts if you want.

If you can't make a deal with a radio station, broadcast your own music with a large sound system. Then the kids can march down the street pantomiming the instruments. *Dave Emmrich*

AS THE STOMACH TURNS

Call it a promotional soap, done in the style of a spontaneous melodrama. Fill in the cost and name of your event towards the end of the script on pages 95-96, then read the narration with shameless pathos. A spontaneous melodrama, by the way, is a no-rehearsal, on-the-spot skit, in which the students—chosen from the audience—act out what the narrator reads. And the more melodramatic and hammy the acting, the better. (For more about spontaneous melodramas—and a collection of them—see *Drama, Skits, & Sketches* in the Ideas Library.) *Ed Stewart*

DORKY CARDS

Is your church blessed with a stash of dorky greeting cards from the '40s and '50s that any self-respecting pastor would be utterly embarrassed to send out? Well they're just stupid enough to work as cards to junior or senior high students.

Send sympathy cards to kids on vacation or who are having the time of their lives at church camp. Get-well cards can be used for students who have achieved stellar success in athletics or academics. *Mike Evans*

WITNESS ADS

Here's a great way to advertise your youth group while giving your kids an opportunity to share their faith in a definite and meaningful way.

Place an ad for your church's youth group in a local high school newspaper, an ad that features the testimony of one of your youths. Ask key kids to write a short statement that they'd like to have published, along with a verse of Scripture. Such an approach will not only promote your group and share the gospel, but will encourage your kids to walk their talk. *Darrel Brock*

Jesus **MAKES THE DIFFERENCE.**

I'm excited God has promised me eternal life because of my personal faith in Jesus Christ. Each day I receive strength to live that day, and I'm blessed by God's abundant love for me. Believe in Jesus . . . have eternal life . . . Jesus really does make the difference. —Joan Brown

"For God loved the world so much that he gave his only Son so that everyone who believes in him should not be lost, but should have eternal life." John 3:16

First Church of South Oak
Dr Morris Swartz, Pastor 1200 Ninth Street, South Oak
Darrel Greene, Minister of Youth

PRESS COVERAGE

You can get hundreds of dollars worth of free publicity if you can learn to think like a newspaper editor. These people are always on the lookout for pictures with seasonal themes.

If your group is planning a Halloween party, a picture of the gang decorating might be usable as a theme picture in your local paper. The picture is valuable only before the event—there isn't great demand for a patriotic theme on July 5. You don't even have to develop the film; the paper can do it easily. Just take the film to the editor (in smaller towns) or the city desk (in larger ones) and tell them what pictures you took. They will carry on from there, but of course the decision about whether to use the picture is theirs alone. They may want you to provide a cut line describing the scene, or they may take down the facts and write their own. *Marion Hostetler*

As the Stomach Turns

A Promotional Spontaneous Melodrama

CHARACTERS
- Narrator
- Lucille Lovelorn (for slapstickish responses, cast a male in this role)
- Philip Pharpar (holds picture frame in front of him)
- Franklin Pharpar
- A door (person standing using fist as doorknob)
- A table (1-2 people on their hands and knees)
- A telephone (person sitting on table using arm as receiver)

PROPS:
- Large picture frame •Ring •Phony check

NARRATOR: And now we present another episode in the continuing life drama, "As the Stomach Turns." Last time, luscious Lucille Lovelorn had spurned Dr. Preakbeak's advances because her precious Philip Pharpar would soon be graduating from law school and they would be married.

Today's scene opens with Lucille standing next to the picture of Philip, which is hanging on the wall of her apartment. Lucille is humming a happy tune to herself as she stares wistfully at the image of her beloved Philip.

"Philip, I miss you so much," she said as she caressed his cheek. "Hurry home to me," she begged, kissing his picture passionately.

Suddenly the telephone rang. Lucille pranced to the table, picked up the receiver, and said sweetly with a smile, "Hello." Then she said, "Oh, Gladys, it's you" and frowned darkly. Philip had found someone new. Philip had told Gladys to tell Lucille goodbye forever for him.

Lucille slammed down the receiver angrily and began to cry. She ran over to the picture of Philip and screamed, "You jerk!" Then she slapped his picture viciously, and began to cry louder. She took the picture of Philip and turned it to the wall and began to cry louder. Then she threw herself on the floor and began to cry louder.

Suddenly, Franklin Pharpar, Philip's younger brother, approached the door and began to knock vigorously. Lucille got up, straightened her hair and skirt, and jerked open the door. Franklin entered the room quickly and said, "Lucille, have you been crying?"

Copyright Youth Specialties, 1224 Greenfield Dr., El Cajon, CA 92021.

"What's it to you, Batface?" pouted Lucille. Then she slapped him painfully across the face. Franklin reached back and slammed the door as viciously as Lucille had slapped him.

"I'm sorry," cried Lucille. Then she began to weep upon his shoulder. "Philip left me," she sobbed as she pointed to the telephone.

"Tommyrot," said Franklin as he stepped back quickly. "He does love you, and he sent me with this for you," he said, holding out a ring. Lucille gave a shriek of joy as she took it from Franklin's hand. Then she gave Franklin a big hug. Lucille leaped to Philip's picture and spun it around to face her.

"I love you, too, darling," she cooed. Then she kissed his picture even more passionately than before. Lucille began dancing around the room with Franklin.

Suddenly the telephone rang again. Lucille skipped to the phone and jerked up the receiver. "Hello, hello, hello," she sang happily. "Oh, Philip, it's you," she sighed dreamily. But then a frown clouded her face: he had found someone else again. They were through.

She slammed down the receiver and angrily threw the ring to the floor. Then she whirled and slapped Franklin.

"You're a liar," she screamed. Then she jumped to Philip's picture. "And *you're* a worthless animal," she shrieked, as she slapped his picture mercilessly. Then she wrenched the picture from the wall and threw it to the floor.

Franklin dropped to one knee and clasped his hands. "But I love you, my flower," he sang. "And I have something more valuable than a ring for you, my pet," he said. Then he pulled a check from his pocket for the amount of $_____. And Lucille knew that here was the supreme gift: he wanted to pay her way to

_____.
name of the activity

Lucille squealed with delight. "What a lovely thought, darling!" she sighed. They embraced happily, then walked across Philip's picture on the floor, and out the door to their new life ahead.

GIANT TICKET

A good way to pump up talk about an event is to print up giant tickets. It is especially effective when an admission fee is charged for the tickets. Results include the following:

• Kids will not only want to buy admission for the event alone, but they will also want to buy the ticket just to have such a novelty.

• It creates an unusual image for your event. Because the ticket is different, kids will believe that the event will probably be different too.

• Kids will talk about it. "Hey, did you buy one of those wild tickets?"

• It makes a great souvenir after the event. Kids bring it to the event for admission, you punch a little hole in it or stamp it, and the kids keep it. It can be hung on a bedroom wall as a reminder of how much fun they had.

The giant ticket can be silk screened at a very low cost. It should be done in two colors, a bright florescent color and a dark color like black. The important thing is that it should look sharp and the bigger the better. Below is a giant ticket used for a film showing at Universal Studios in Hollywood. The really wild thing was seeing 200 youth direc-

tors show up at Universal with these huge florescent tickets. Also, because everyone had something in common (a giant ticket), it helped people meet, laugh, and talk together, even though they had never met. The giant ticket is especially good for banquets, grad parties, and events where people have a tendency to be extra proper and formal.

YOUTH GROUP ANNUAL

Begin a local youth group annual or yearbook. Have someone take pictures of youth group happenings. Someone else can report newsworthy items to your local newspaper and later clip these new articles. Obtain a large three-ring notebook with acetate-covered sheets. Mount the articles and pictures. These can effectively advertise coming events and provide your youth group members with fun memories. Include the names of your youth group officers, retreat committee, sponsors, special recognition awards, etc. *Ed Bender*

BUS BENCH BACKS

Many cities rent bus bench backs for advertising. A church youth group or coffeehouse can rent this space for a remarkably reasonable rate in many cities. *Jim Ramsey*

CAMPUS VISITS

One way to make campus visits less intimidating is to distribute pictures of your students from recent youth events. Have double prints made of photos taken at various activities and take one set with you to the school. When you see students who attended these events, give them pictures that feature them. They'll love it. Their friends will want to see the pictures, too, and will ask all about the events. Kids will look forward to seeing you—or at least your pictures. *John Wood*

Psst! Hey, wanna make some money? For a service project? Road trip? For a missionary? Or just need to bulk up your youth budget a bit? Here are sales and auctions, pledge-a-thons and food events. Even quirky jobs that people will actually *pay* you for—like washing golf clubs at the local links (page 106), airplanes at municipal airports (108), or chaperoning the children of harried parents at fairs (107).

FOODS & FUN

CARHOP FRY OUT

As a fundraiser and special event, have the youth group grill hamburgers, hot dogs, etc., in the parking lot and invite the community to come and eat. The kids serve as carhops and wait on people in their cars, taking their orders and bringing the food. Desserts, drinks and other items should be on the menu as well. *Roger Voskuil*

FAMILY FUN

Put on the World's Craziest Basketball Game, featuring the youth group versus the adults of the church. Sell tickets, award door prizes, provide concessions, the whole works. The game will prove to be a ton of laughs and good for involving families in some great fellowship. Make it an annual affair and watch the attendance and excitement grow. *Ken Bowers*

BAGEL BREAKFAST

Preparing and delivering pre-sold bagel breakfasts requires some legwork, but the fun and profit to your youth group make it worthwhile.

Choose a Sunday for delivering the breakfasts. Well ahead of the event, get the kids together to plan a breakfast menu. An easy meal could include one quart of milk, one quart of orange juice, four croissants and four bagels, and a copy of the Sunday paper of your choice. Try asking the supervisor of a paper delivery person in your group for free copies for the day of your event. Together create a logo expressing the purpose of the fundraiser. Use this logo for publicity and later on grocery sacks to be filled and delivered for breakfast. Plan a big promotion for the fundraiser. Schedule announcement dates and opportunities to sell the breakfast to members of the congregation, as well as to friends and neighbors.

Set a cost for the meal—the cost for the above meal, for example, could be $15. Assign several kids and a sponsor to approach local grocery stores to request a price break on the purchase of the milk and juice and to seek out a bakery that might do the same for the breads. When merchants discover you are attempting to raise money for neighborhood youths (your youth group), they are often willing to help. The profit margin can be as high as 100 percent. Finally, make a plan for distribution of the breakfasts on the designated Sunday.

On the Saturday before you deliver the breakfasts, meet with the kids to purchase or pick up the needed products, to decorate the delivery bags with the logo, and to assign delivery teams for the next day. On Sunday after church, the kids can distribute as many of the breakfasts as possible to church members at the service and deliver the remainder to homes in the afternoon. A group of three to five kids will make delivery to a defined geographical area both fun and efficient.

If the event is worth repeating annually, the legwork decreases as people know what to expect and have already helped you in the past. *Bradley Bergfalk*

SPUD NITE

Net profits of $500 and more have been realized by groups that conduct this easy fundraiser. Check with a restaurant supplier in order to get the largest potatoes, and then farm them out to students' homes to bake. For a $5 advance-sale ticket, people get a potato, drink, dessert—and best of all, their choice of toppings, set out in lavish buffet-fashion. The more toppings, the better!

Here are the quantities you'll need to feed 200 people:

- 215 potatoes
- 10 lbs. cheddar cheese (grated)
- 10 lbs. onions (chopped)
- 10 lbs. mushrooms (sliced)
- 1 gal. salad dressing (ranch)
- 24 family-size tea bags
- 1 gal. crouton/potato topping mix
- 10 lbs. margarine spread
- 10 lbs. sour cream
- 1 lb. bacon bits
- 8 lbs. hamburger meat
- 2 oz. freeze-dried chopped chives
- 2 cans (#10) cheese sauce (nacho and cheddar)
- 1 can (#10) chili
- 3 bags chili beans
- 3 lbs. frozen broccoli
- 4 cans chopped green chilies
- 9 heads lettuce
- 1 lug tomatoes
- Lots of aluminum foil

The skit on page 103 works great for publicity. Perform it during announcements in the worship service or another time when the congregation is assembled.

On the actual Spud Nite, add some Christian music to the mix—either live or taped—and you'll have a dining adventure that your church will beg you to repeat in a few months. *Keith Lorry and Don Orange*

ALTERNATIVE DINING

This fundraiser has generated hundreds of dollars for youth groups—and it's a people pleaser too. Simply fix dinner for the congregation after the morning service. Keep it simple—sloppy joes, spaghetti, or chili for the main dish, carrot and celery sticks, deli salads, chips, cookies—and bill it as "Alternative Dining: No cooking, no mess, no fast food, no cold pizza, no program, no long lines."

The congregation can trickle in whenever they're finished visiting after the service and can leave whenever they want. No tickets, either—just a donation box at the door. Don't worry—youth groups from modest-sized churches have netted at least two to three hundred dollars per meal. Just keep the line moving and bring seconds to the tables for the patrons. Teens can cook, set up, clean up, serve, hold little ones, and act as hosts and hostesses.

Once you serve them like this, your church may demand Alternative Dining every month! *Linda Miller*

Spud Nite
Fundraiser Commercial

CHARACTERS
•Youth group sponsor •Youth group student

SPONSOR: Say, *(name of youth group member)*, I heard about your cool fundraiser called Spud Nite. When is it?

STUDENT: *(with no enthusiasm)* Oh, it's on _____ *(day of the week)* night, _____ *(date)* from _____ *(beginning time)* to _____ *(ending time)* at _____ *(location)*.

SPONSOR: You sure don't sound very excited about it. What's the problem?

STUDENT: Well, you know we've put up with lots of our youth worker's crazy ideas, but this one is the worst. "Spud Nite." That sounds like something they do in Idaho. I don't think many _____ *(the term for citizens of your state)* are going to come to something called "Spud Nite."

SPONSOR: What?! Nobody come to Spud Nite? These just aren't your ordinary potatoes, bud. These baked beauties will be covered with your choice of delicious toppings—nacho cheese, cheddar cheese, chili, tomatoes, beans, broccoli, mushrooms, sour cream, butter, bacon, hamburger, onions. These are no common tators, I can guarantee that. Trust me—this spud's for you. Besides, a lot of people in this church love potatoes. Why, they grew up with potatoes at every meal. In fact, most of these people are part potato.

STUDENT: What do you mean they're part potato?

SPONSOR: Well, when I look over this crowd, I see all sorts of potatoes.

STUDENT: Like where?

SPONSOR: Look at the guy back there. See him? His name is DICK TATOR. He'll command his wife to take a night off and go to Spud Nite.

STUDENT: Really?

SPONSOR: Yeah. And look over there. That guy's name is COMMON TATOR. He's always got something to explain to you. He'll be there because he'll want something to talk about next Sunday morning after church.

STUDENT: Okay, I think I see a tator out there.

SPONSOR: Good! You're catching on quick. Where's your tator?

STUDENT: Right...there. She's HESI TATOR. She's not sure she wants to come. What did you say would be on those potatoes at Spud Nite?

SPONSOR: *(loudly)* I said, "These baked beauties will be covered with your choice of delicious toppings—nacho cheese, cheddar cheese, chili, tomatoes, broccoli, mushrooms, sour cream, butter, bacon, hambur—"

STUDENT: Not so loud!

SPONSOR: Why not?

STUDENT: You'll wake up MEDI TATOR here in the front row.

SPONSOR: Sorry.

STUDENT: You know, _____ *(name of sponsor)*, the more I think about Spud Nite and the more I look at this great group of people here, the more I really think we will have a great turnout.

TOGETHER: *(to the audience)* Come out and support the _____ *(youth group name)* fundraiser next week. Don't crash in front of the TV and veg out. Don't sit out in the parking lot, like SPEC TATOR there. Instead, be like IMMY TATOR and follow everyone else to the _____ *(place, date, time)* for a night your taste spuds will never forget!

END

Le Grande Chateau

The idea is to open—for one night only—your own fine French restaurant—an elegant dining experience that includes classy entertainment. The whole thing, however, is done slightly tongue-in-cheek. The catch is the small print at the bottom of the menu that reads: "Management reserves the right to make substitutions without patron consent." So regardless of what people order, they all get the same thing.

Le Chateau Grande

Entrees
Includes dinner roll, dessert, and hot beverage

Storione a la Cardinale
$15.55

New York Steak
$19.20

Veal Marengo and Gamberi
$17.60

Dumpling Dewar Stew
$12.00

Bigginacca de Ronaldois
$18.90

Fischer Fried Chicken
$12.75

Arthur's Perogy Geschmack
$19.00

Lobster Waikiki
$28.65
(children's portions available upon request)

Appetizers $8.00 ea.
Escargot
Galettes au Fromage
Canapes
Frog's Legs
Bongo Bongo

Floor shows commence at 7:30 & 9:30 p.m.
Management reserves the right to make substitutions without patron consent.

The menu should be elaborate and include extravagant dishes at high prices. It should look like a regular menu—with the exception of the catch line at the bottom, of course. The publicity should include a snooty by-reservation-only system so the right amount of food can be prepared. You can also have a dress code—ties for the gentlemen, please. Decorations should be as elegant as possible, with cut flowers, candlelight, linen on the tables, and classical music playing in the background.

The waiters should be dressed to the hilt, with the maitre d' in tux if possible. The food should be nice but simple. Juice, tossed salad, baked chicken, baked potato, vegetable, roll, dessert. The program after the meal can be anything you want. Be sure to allow a few minutes to explain your project and how the proceeds of the evening will be used.

At the close, the waiters can present the cheque to each customer. It can instruct people to make their donations in any amount and to pay their waiter or pay on their way out. Usually a special event like this gets very good results. It's worth all the work involved. *Len Kageler*

Delightful Desserts

As the holiday season approaches, your group can raise funds by advertising delightful desserts for sale. Simply distribute a list of baked goodies which your youths, their parents, and others in the congregation would be willing to bake and donate. Then take orders. This way you know ahead of time exactly how many items you'll sell, and you'll avoid the confusion of baking too many or too few goodies. Since baked goods are donated, the receipts are pure profit. *Kaye Carew*

Macho Bake Sale

Bake sales have always been successful fundraisers, but here it is with a new twist. Get all the men in the church to bake cakes, cookies, and pies, and have a Macho Bake Sale. You might even want to make it a contest among the men; no women may help them. It will be a lot of fun, generate a lot of enthusiasm, and work great as a fundraiser. *Rick Bell*

DONUT SALE

For an easy source of funds, have youth group members serve donuts and coffee each Sunday before and after the morning worship service. The donuts can either be donated, bought at wholesale, or homemade. The people then buy the donuts for the going price, just enough that the youth group can make a little on each one sold. To expand the offerings, you could also offer bagels, orange juice, and milk. Most people really enjoy a treat in the morning at church and are happy to pay for it. *Malcolm McQueen*

AFTER-CHURCH SALAD BAR

While many youth groups provide coffee and donuts for churchgoers, this idea involves a salad bar instead. It's easy to do, and the adults love it. Have teens purchase and prepare the ingredients—lettuce, tomatoes, mushrooms, sprouts, radishes, sunflower seeds, salad dressings, etc.— and set the salad bar up in the fellowship area after the service. People can pay a set price for the salad bar or just make a contribution of any amount to the youth group. *Dave Hick*

GRANOLA PARTY

Most people can really sink their teeth into this idea. Get the youth group together for a granola party at which the kids make their own special brand of granola to sell later. Find a good recipe—preferably one that includes lots of good stuff such as nuts, banana chips, carob chips, coconut, grains, honey, and the like. Have the kids prepare the granola in large quantities, then bag it, put it in decorated coffee cans, and sell it door to door or to friends and relatives. You could expand the offerings and also make jam, preserves, dried fruit, or other natural foods.

BAKE-IN

Here's a good fundraiser for teens who like all-night activities. It's a combination lock-in/bake-off/bake sale. The group gathers at the church at 10:00 p.m. (possibly after a ball game or other activity) to start preparations for the night. All the flour, sugar, eggs, milk, and other ingredients should already be in place for the event. These ingredients could be purchased, but it is best to get members of your church to donate items and/or check with stores and distributors about donating or selling broken packages or old shelf items that are still usable.

Several weeks in advance, youth group members advertise this event and circulate order blanks that list all the items you will be baking. With your orders in hand, there's nothing left to do but start in. Hopefully, you will have several moms or others in the church who are experienced cooks to help with this project. Items that are baked during the night can be either delivered to the purchaser's door or picked up the following morning. Payment should be made on delivery or pick-up.

Teens get a great deal of satisfaction from this kind of a project as they see people enjoying the fruits of their labors, and as they benefit from added funds for the church youth program. Here are some suggested offerings: Apple and cherry strudel, banana nut bread, donuts, coffee cake, cinnamon rolls, white or wheat bread, zucchini bread, cupcakes, chocolate chip cookies, sugar cookies, banana cream pie, chocolate pie, etc. The project will go over great if you can keep from eating what you bake before it's sold! *Dwight Douglas*

RECIPE FUNDRAISER

The youth group collects recipes from anyone in or out of the church, organizes them into sections, and prints them with contributor's name at the

---

Recipe Form

Your Name: _____
Address and Phone Number: _____
_____

Title of Recipe: _____
Category: (soup, main dish, dessert, etc.) _____

Ingredients: _____
_____
_____
_____

Preparation: _____
_____
_____

Yield: _____

---

bottom of the page. The recipes are copied or printed and put in a semi-hard or hardcover notebook. You can sell them for a profit. *Ron Wells*

PANCAKE WASH

Combine a pancake breakfast with a car wash! People pay one price for both. They bring their car in for a wash. Then while they are waiting, they go inside the church for a pancake breakfast. When they return, their car is spanking clean. *Bill Robinson*

HANDS FOR HIRE

GOLF CLUB WASH

This unusual fundraiser works well in a community with at least one golf course and avid golfers. Set up a booth at the 18th green of a local golf course and offer to wash golf clubs for the tired hackers. All you need is permission from the golf course pro (or park board for municipal courses), a pail of soapy water, a brush, a pail of clean water, a coin collector, and a few towels. For extra service, offer to wax the woods and use a metal polish on the irons. If the money is going to a worthy cause, most golfers will be glad to pay a reasonable price. *Warren Ueckert*

YOUTH LEADER LOTTERY

You can be the grand prize in a youth group lottery. Have the kids buy lottery tickets, with your services for a day or evening as the prize. For example, you could be the winner's butler for a Saturday, or wash windows, or anything else you might conjure up that will be within limits. Be sure to set the boundaries before the lottery begins.

A spin-off of this idea might be to sponsor a community event—a concert or party—around Christmas in which the admission ticket also serves as a lottery ticket to be drawn sometime during the evening. The winner would get an all-expense-paid date, with you serving as personal chauffeur/chaperon for the night. In fact, expanding the pool of lottery participants this way will give some extra exposure to your ministry. *Chuck Behrens*

TASK-TRADIN' TICKET

Sell coupons like the ones pictured below for a fast and fun fundraiser. Tickets entitle buyers to an hour of work from the student seller. You may want to design two tickets—one with a higher purchase price for more strenuous work or more than one hour of work, and one with a lower price for easier work or just an hour of work. *Michael Gulotta*

HIRE A SUPERKID

Run an employment service for your youth group. Most unemployed young people have lots of time on their hands after school and on weekends. You and your church can help them to find good part-time jobs that provide meaningful work and can raise money for teens and for the youth group.

To make it happen, print up an attractive flier that includes information on odd jobs that the kids can do: mow yards, wash cars, baby-sit, clean house, paint, fix cars, etc. Distribute the fliers all over the neighborhood and wait for the calls to start coming in. Chances are your response will be very good.

When responses to the flier come in, assign kids to jobs that match their abilities and preferences. Give them the responsibility for completing the

---

TASK TRADIN' TICKET

Minimum donation: $5
This ticket entitles the bearer to 1 hour of work from the youth-group member whose signature is below:

Student's signature: _____

Student's phone number: _____
(See reverse for work agreement)

This ticket is not transferable
All arrangements for the completion of one hour of work will be made between the student and the bearer of this ticket. No unreasonably strenuous work beyond the student's capacity will be demanded. All proceeds from this ticket will be used for_____.
(name of function).
This ticket must be used before _____.
(date)

First Church Youth Group

chores and doing a good job. If customers are satisfied, chances are good that they will become regular customers. When the jobs start thinning out, send out more fliers or get some other free publicity.

Employers can pay the young people or the youth group. You might want to work out a system where a percentage of the money goes toward the youth group project, and the rest is kept by the young people for their own use. *John Collins*

RENT-A-RIDER

If county fair time is a big weekend of the summer in your area, this fundraiser not only fills empty youth group coffers, but spells relief for moms and dads who aren't up to taking their kids on a dozen stomach-churning carnival rides.

Near the main ticket booths, rent booth space where parents can rent a high schooler for $10 a half day, plus ride tickets for junior and the teen. To many parents, ten bucks is a small price to pay for a big brother or sister to accompany the kids on rides and generally keep them in tow. You can prorate the cost for shorter periods of time, but most parents are eager to opt for the whole package.

The children are delighted to finally get on those rides they've never been allowed on before; parents are relieved they can sit out this year's rides; and your youth group members don't mind being in charge a kid for a few hours—especially when they can ride the Octopus for free! *Bob Baker*

DOOR-TO-DOOR CAR WASH

Send your kids out in groups of two or three armed with buckets, sponges, rags, soap, and squeegees. Instruct them as they go door-to-door to assure car owners that to have their cars washed, all they need to supply is the water. The convenience of an in-your-own-driveway car wash usually yields generous donors. *Lynn H. Pryor*

DOGGIE DIP

For an unusual fundraiser that would work with any size youth group, try having a Doggie Dip. Advertise that your youth group will wash pet dogs on a certain Saturday for a small fee. Most dog owners hate to wash their dogs, so the response will undoubtedly be tremendous.

Get together lots of metal or plastic tubs, some dog shampoo, towels, and hoses—and be ready for everything from bloodhounds to beagles. *Mike and Donna Younus*

FAIRGROUNDS CLEAN-UP

This profitable and dependable fundraiser can become an annual project for your youth group. Contract with your local fairgrounds, stadium, or parade organizer to do clean-up after a major event. The job usually takes about a day and a half and can earn hundreds of dollars. With good organization and teamwork, this kind of job doesn't have to be overwhelming, and good work will pay off in getting next year's contract. *Robert Crosby*

Car Wash Incentives

Car washes are a popular way to raise money for youth group projects. They are usually easy to organize and a lot of fun for the kids to do. The best way to make the car wash profitable is to sell advance tickets. All kids in the youth group get a stack of tickets to sell during the weeks prior to the car wash date. Most people will buy a ticket even if they are unable to bring their car in for a wash.

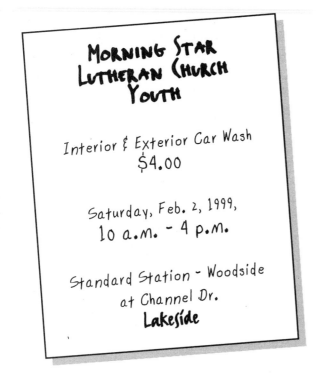

MORNING STAR
LUTHERAN CHURCH
YOUTH

Interior & Exterior Car Wash
$4.00

Saturday, Feb. 2, 1999,
10 a.m. - 4 p.m.

Standard Station - Woodside
at Channel Dr.
Lakeside

Is your car wash is to help defray the costs of summer camp or some other activity that requires each kid to come up with a certain amount of money? Here's a good way to allocate the money fairly and provide incentive for the students to sell tickets. For every advance-sale ticket, kids receive half the ticket price off their camp registration fee. For example, if a kid sold 10 tickets at $4 each, he or she receives $20 off the cost of camp. So the more tickets they sell, the less it costs them personally to go to camp. This is whether they are able to help wash cars or not.

On the day of the actual car wash, the kids who are washing cars have a chance to earn the other half of the ticket price. For every ticket that is redeemed, the students washing cars at the time get the other half of the price divided equally among them. For any car washes sold on location—people who just drive in to get their car washed—all of that money goes to the students washing cars at that time. If a ticket is not redeemed, then half of the ticket price goes to overhead, transportation, or whatever.

A system such as this ensures that all students receive the benefit of their actual contributions. All money should be turned in to the youth director or treasurer for allocation. The kids should not handle the money themselves or keep the money. Chances are they will wind up spending it before camp rolls around. All money that comes in reduces the cost of camp. Obviously, this system requires some record keeping and mathematics, but it's pretty fair. *Dave Griewe*

A Good Clean Job

If your youth group has trouble raising money, perhaps they can do as one group did. They became the church custodians. Custodians are usually hard to obtain and often underpaid. With a good-sized group, the job can be done in a short time and in a very adequate manner. This approach is sometimes better than trying to sell things or beg for bucks. *Daniel Unrath*

Group Inventory

Call large retail stores in your city and volunteer for group inventory. Every store has to take a periodic inventory and usually needs temporary help to do it. They'll pay at least minimum wage, which can be a good fundraiser for the youth group if the kids agree to kick in their pay. *Richard McPherson*

Airplane Wash

As a possible fund raiser, contact your local airport for private planes and inquire into the possibility of having a plane wash. Airplane owners will usually pay plenty to have their plane washed. All it requires is plenty of hose, buckets, rags, towels, soap, and kids to do the work. All it takes is a few airplanes to make the effort very worthwhile.

AUCTIONS & SALES

MEAL OF FORTUNE

This fundraiser auction allows members of your church to participate as buyers, sellers, or both. Place a box in the church where people can leave a card with a brief description of a special meal they would be willing to prepare and serve in their home for the highest bidder. These may be anything from enticing specialty dishes to grilled hamburgers. Church members can submit as many meal plans as they like, and for each they should say how many people they could serve—two, four, or whatever. They should also note whether or not children would be welcome.

Then, after a Sunday service, the meals can be auctioned off to the highest bidder without telling who will be preparing each one. After the auction, the buyer and seller agree on a convenient time when they could enjoy the meal together. All proceeds are collected at the time of the auction, and everything collected is profit. Best of all, this approach provides more opportunities for fellowship among church members. *Ruth Holste*

CELEBRITY PARAPHERNALIA AUCTION

If you're willing to do some research and invest $25 or $30 in postage, you can make nearly $1,000 with this idea. Several months before the fundraiser itself, comb through your Christian music CDs, tapes, and albums for the addresses of artists' management, ministries, or agencies. Also phone your local Christian radio station to get addresses of popular Christian authors, speakers, preachers, and comedians. For the addresses of movie and TV stars, sport celebrities, and singers, spend an afternoon in a library poring over Who's Who Among Celebrities.

Once you have a list of people and addresses, you're ready to do some letter writing. Round up your youth group to spend an evening writing letters, stuffing envelopes, and licking stamps. The letters should follow this general line: You are raising funds for your church youth group and would appreciate donated, autographed items for an upcoming auction. After you send the letters, sit back and wait. Your work is done—until auction time, that is.

Within several weeks, you'll probably begin receiving lots of mail from big-time celebs—autographed albums, pictures, T-shirts, books, cassettes. It's not unusual to realize a response rate of nearly 50 percent.

Now it's auction time! Obtain the services of a humorous auctioneer and a lovely assistant to display the merchandise. Then during a church-wide, after-service fellowship—during which your kids serve fancy mints and nuts—sell the stuff to the highest bidders. *Doug King*

TIME, TALENT, AND GOODS AUCTION

To raise funds, you can auction off not only items, but special services provided by both youth and adults in the church. Each young person should donate three or four items—garage-sale type items, homemade pies, or hand-crafted gifts—and services—such as baby-sitting or yard work. Others in the congregation can volunteer to do the same. Your youths might even work together with the men's and women's groups in the church to make some items; the time they spend together will probably be as valuable as the auction itself.

Six or eight weeks before the event, publicize a list of items and services to be auctioned, along with the initial bidding price for each. If you can, display some of the items in the church ahead of time so folks can see what they're bidding on.

The night of the auction, persons interested in bidding register their names and receive an auction card with a number on it. Youth workers at the registration table keep track of who buys what. Have one or two adults act as auctioneers. Serving refreshments adds a nice touch and provides additional fundraising. At the end of the evening, buyers pay for their purchases at the registration table as they leave. *Bob Machovec*

Musical Bake Sale

This fusion of ideas can be a big moneymaker for your group and lots of fun for your church. Have your group make cakes and baked goods for an auction or sale and calculate the cost. Next, gather donated music cassettes, CDs, and videos. Wrap the items in foil, place a cake next to each foil-wrapped item, place one price sticker in front of each pair of items, and auction them off to the highest bidder.

You'll make a profit, and buyers will enjoy their cakes and music. Alternatively, sell candy instead of baked goods. *Jim Burton*

Potluck Auction

Sponsor a potluck dinner and invite your entire congregation to attend. Kids in your group whose last names begin with letters A to L can bring a main dish and dessert; the M to Zers can bring a salad and dessert. Also provide coffee and punch. Your teens are also responsible for serving and clean-up.

Ask each family to bring along a gift to be auctioned off—special cakes or pies, other baked goods, hand-crafted items, or household goods of some value. Place these items on a table and invite everyone to browse during the dinner hour and view the items for auction.

When the tables are cleared, begin to auction off each item, saving the most expensive for last. If there is someone in your church with auctioneer experience, try to take advantage of that. Otherwise, find a person who can humorously generate lots of enthusiasm for every item. *Linda Behrendt*

Candy Sales

If your group is thinking of selling candy as a fundraising project, check with a local candy wholesaler as a supplier. Often a local dealer can save you more money than a fundraising company, and still obtain fundraiser-size items for you to sell. Just look in the yellow pages under Candy Wholesalers. *Richard Everett*

Sample Fair

This idea takes a few months to get ready for, but it is very effective as a fundraiser, and different enough to attract a lot of attention. The first step is to write a form letter (see sample) to various companies that provide products, foods, or services. Send the letter to nationally known or local companies. You might want to contact some of these companies personally with a phone call or visit. In the letter ask them to give you a large quantity of free samples for your sample fair.

Dear Business Leader:

Would you like us to promote your product?

Our senior high youth group has decided to raise money to purchase a video camera for our church. We are calling our project a Sample Fair. In order for it to be a success, we are asking for your help. In return we will help you promote your product.

Here is our request: Will you donate samples of your product? We will not sell these samples directly; rather we will sell tickets in advance and at the door to the sample fair. Our goal is to sell 300 tickets. Each ticket holder will receive one of each sample that companies such as yours make available. To complete the evening, the teens will present a talent show.

We're certain the samples will generate interest and excitement, and we will have a good turnout.

This event will take place on March 18 in our church fellowship room. We would be very pleased to receive your samples.

Thank you very much.

Sincerely,

Make sure your letterhead has your church's complete name, address, and phone number. Also provide the phone number of the contact person if the number is different from the church number.

If you send a letter like this to enough companies, you can get hundreds of different free samples. Tickets to the fair can be sold for whatever price you feel is reasonable. Arrange to have your teens distribute the samples at the fair—one per customer. Some companies may provide plastic bags for people to collect things in, or they may send a representative to present the product to ticket holders. At any rate the overhead is low and the benefits are high. You can also provide a refreshment booth or sell baked goods, etc. to add to the festivities. It can be a fun evening that raises a lot of money for a worthwhile cause. *Esther Maule*

ALLEY SALE

For this unique variation of the garage sale, it's best to find an alley with four to eight garages that you can borrow. Each garage becomes a different shop named according to the merchandise sold in it. One shop can sell household items; another can sell sports equipment; others can sell antiques, books, clothing or baked goods, etc. Give each shop a clever name—like the shops in a mall—and post signs at each end of the alley to call attention to this unique shopping experience.

Preparation for this event is crucial to its success. You will need to enlist many people to donate items for sale. Merchandise will have to be collected, sorted, and priced. Advertise through newspaper ads, public service announcements on the radio, etc. Workers on the day of the sale will to do the actual selling, parking cars, directing traffic, etc. The atmosphere should be as festive as possible. You might even get some musicians to play at one end of the alley and some jugglers or clowns to perform at the other end. Use your own creativity to design an event that will attract the most people possible.

If you can't find an alley of this type, select a normal street, using front lawns or garages off the street. This event works so well that you may want to make it an annual event. *Elizabeth J. Sandell*

CRAZY AUCTION

This alternative auction works best with a rather large group. An article of value is put up for bid and the bidder starts at five cents. The person who bid the nickel tosses in this five cents immediately upon making the bid. The auctioneer announces that the five-cent bid has been paid and then raises the bidding to 10 cents. The one who bids 10 cents tosses in the dime as a firm commitment of his or her intention. The auctioneer tries to raise the bidding and someone may bid a quarter, whereupon the 25 cents gets tossed in, making the total in the pot 40 cents. The bidding continues until no one bids again and then the article goes to the last person to bid. All of the previously paid money stays in the pot as well as the final bid. It is easy to sell a pair of shoes for two dollars when there is actually 11 dollars in the pot. *Larry Houseman*

JUNK AUCTION

Have fun and raise money for your group at the same time by collecting a lot of interesting junk that you think your kids would want to buy. Then auction it off to your group. You'll be surprised at what kids will buy and at what they're willing to spend. Develop funny, creative auction routines to sell the items to your crowd. This works best with a large group. When the bidding is good, the results are hilarious.

TALENTS FOR SALE

GAME LEADERS FOR HIRE

Train your youth group to stage and execute adventure games for other groups and events to raise money. *David Boshart*

SINGING VALENTINE

Here is a good fundraiser that works best on Valentine's Day. The youth group simply invites everyone in the congregation to purchase secretly a valentine for their sweethearts on the Sunday before Valentine's Day. You can charge somewhere around $5 per valentine.

Then on Valentine's Day, the youth group arrives at each sweetheart's house and delivers the surprise singing valentine. The group should all be dressed in red and several members can be dressed as Cupid. The group can either write fun love songs or sing some well-known ones. After singing—which can be both romantic and silly—the sweetheart can be presented with a Certificate of Affection with the secret admirer's name on it. This activity can also involve delivery of flowers and/or candy for extra cost. The elderly and shut-ins especially appreciate receiving a surprise singing valentine. *Ann C. Swallow*

SCREEN-PRINTED T-SHIRTS

Printed T-shirts and sweatshirts are a modern art form, a fashion, a display of teen talents, and a walking billboard for anything and everything—including your youth group. Printed sportswear helps build group unity for choir tours, mission projects, and other special events. It is also a reminder of the event and a conversation piece that extends an event's ministry by months to those who see the shirt and ask the wearer about its meaning. But more than this, screen-printed shirts have great fundraising potential!

With three or four teens helping, you can print a shirt every thirty seconds, once you get the hang of it. Buying plain shirts wholesale and using your youth group for creativity and labor means you can make a healthy profit and still undersell the professional printers. Who do you sell to? All sorts of groups are looking for custom printed shirts—church softball leagues, denominational district events, pro-life marches, and other church groups in your area, for starters.

Here's where to start: the Hunt Manufacturing company sells an inexpensive shirt-printing kit that gives you everything you need to get started. Kits sell in the $45-$80 range and are available at most graphic-arts supply stores. If you cannot find it, call Hunt's toll-free number, 1-800-879-4868, for a distributor of Hunt-Speedball materials in your area.

About buying T-shirts: You don't need to spend amount that retailers charge per shirt. There are lots of wholesalers around the country from whom you can buy shirts, sweats, jackets, hats, and all kinds of other printable items for ridiculously low prices. For instance, you can get most brands and colors of T-shirts for $2.50 to $3.50 apiece when you buy them in lots of a dozen. Here are a few suppliers to get you started:
• Eisner Bros. in New York at 1-8426-7700
• Southern California Ts at 1-800-829-5000
• T-Shirts West, Inc. in Colorado at 1-800-543-4006
• The Predot Co. in Louisiana at 1-800-422-8860
• Indiana Ts at 1-800-767-9696

With a little snooping around, you can find other suppliers of both clothing and printing materials. Mail order is the key to getting the best prices. Then all you need is a little cutting and pasting, a sheet of rub-on letters or a computer-printer-software combination with graphics capability, a little artistic talent, and access to a photocopier that can generate overhead transparencies—and you can produce some snappy artwork. *David Shaw*

CRAFTS BOUTIQUE

Crafts and handmade items are very popular. There is no doubt that many people in your church or community are talented at making things that will sell in a boutique or gift shop. So, why not set up a crafts boutique to help finance your next mission project? Pick a good location, advertise it well, and invite everyone to make something in the arts and crafts motif and to allow these items to be sold on a consignment basis. You can buy the items from them at a wholesale price, with the profit going to support your project. Some people may be willing to donate their crafts items.

One church did this in a big way, and on a weekend sold over $20,000 worth of goods. A fixed percentage of the income went to the mission project, and the rest went to the people who had made and sold the items. Needless to say, it was very successful.

PLEDGE-A-THONS

PINS FOR MISSIONS

Secure the use of a bowling alley and set up a bowling tournament or just an evening of bowling with your young people. The object is to raise money for a worthy cause by taking pledges from adults and business people in the community. Each kid enlists the help of sponsors who pledge a certain amount of money—a nickle, a dime, a quarter, or more—for each point scored while bowling. Kids bowl three games, and their total points determine the amount of their sponsors' pledges. In a tournament, the winners continue scoring more points, therefore collecting more money for the cause. One group called the event Pins for Missions and used their money for world missions. *David Peters*

ROCK-A-THON

A 24-hour Rock-a-Thon involves everyone in the group. Participants enlist sponsors at a certain amount for every hour spent rocking in a rocking chair. Here are the rules:
• Contestants provide their own rocking chairs.
• Participants must rock at least four hours in succession.
• Time breaks are allowed only for trips to the bathroom.
• Chairs must be moving at all times.

Hold the event in a large room and supply television, stereos, coffee, cookies, and lemonade. Keep the participants awake by cheering and a lot of cold, wet towels. Meals can be provided by the church, families, or whatever. Also, keep track of total funds raised every four or five hours and announce it to the kids. It keeps enthusiasm high.

After participants finish rocking, they are given an official time certificate to show their sponsors. Keep a master record on all participants and their times to make sure all money is collected. Take lots of pictures, and invite a local television station to film the event. *Dick Stiansen*

IN-LOCK THON-A-ROCK

Here's a good event for February 29th or any other day. It's a crazy backward event, the In-Lock Thon-a-Rock. It's a lock-in and a Rock-a-Thon done backwards. A lock-in is a weekend activity in which the students bring sleeping bags, etc. and campout inside the church, and a Rock-a-Thon is a fundraiser that involves rocking in rocking chairs for a long time.

To do it backwards, kids should come with their clothes on backwards, walk in backwards, say goodbye as they enter, and so on. Play some games backwards, have breakfast in the evening, sit backwards in the rockers and count the hours backwards (start with 10 or so, and end with none). Think creatively on this and it can be a lot of fun. *Steve Burgener*

SERVICE ROCK-A-THON

A new dimension is added to the Rock-a-Thon idea when the youth pledge an hour of service for every hour they rock. For example if 20 youth rock for 12 hours, the entire group pledges 240 hours or service. The group can then work off the time by visiting shut-ins, going on service retreats and work camps, doing yard work for the disabled, etc. Of course, you still get adult sponsors to give a certain amount of money per hour rocked, but the adults are much more willing to pledge if they know the youth are going to work and give something themselves. *Elaine Rowe*

BUCK-A-BASKET GAME

A basketball game that pits two rival teams against each other can be fun and effective. Take pledges from people to give a buck-a-basket scored by their favorite team. The game can be regulation time and open to the public.

A variation of this would be to make it a marathon game, lasting as long as the players can continue. Donors may pledge a penny-a-point, based on the total number of points scored by both teams. The more points scored, the more money raised. In other words, if the teams played continuously for eight hours, scoring a total of 1250 points, then each donor would pay $12.50. Of course, pledges can be more—like the buck-a-basket—but people may give as much as they feel they are able. If people know ahead of time that the funds are being raised for a worthy project, the response will normally be greater. *Robin Williams*

WRITE-A-THON

Have your group sign up sponsors with the promise that the teens will conduct an all-night Write-a-Thon: they'll stay up all night writing encouraging letters to youth groups at other churches, to ministers, to college students from their group, to missionaries, relatives, community leaders, members of Congress, etc.

Because letters can be written quickly, the pledges should probably be smaller than usual—maybe five to ten cents a letter. If a teen writes 75 letters in one night—which isn't unusual—that's about a $4 to $8 pledge. Use your church's bulk-rate mailing permit to save on postage. *Doug Rice*

SHAVE-A-THON

For this fundraiser you'll need to recruit as many men as you can—male youth sponsors, guys from the college group, etc.—who are both of serious shaving age and willing to go without shaving for two to three weeks. You want real tough-looking male faces that girls will bid big bucks for in order to shave!

On the day of the Shave-a-Thon, have all sorts of razors, shaving cream, and aftershave ready. Then auction off the guys to be shaved by the highest bidding girls. With every sort of shaving cream and razor at their disposal, they can chop away to their hearts' delight—and many men will walk away with tissue pieces stuck to their faces. And look out—if the men feel they've sacrificed too much of their faces—this entertaining fundraiser may end with a shaving-cream fight! *Rox Riendeau*

SCRIPTURE-A-THON

This fundraiser has spiritual benefits for your group as well as financial ones.

Challenge your teens to memorize Scripture. Distribute lists of 30 to 50 individual verses, whole psalms or chapters, portions of Scripture, or a mixture of these. Give your group a two- or three-month time frame. During this time, youths solicit folks in your congregation to sponsor them—in this case, for a set amount of money per verse memorized. Many people in your church will be eager to support such a contest.

When it comes time for payment, sponsors have the right to ask kids to quote the verses they have learned, with Scripture references, of course—book, chapter, verse. Alternatively, you could make the day

or night of verse recitation a big deal—a party or a contest, open to the congregation or just the group. Keep track of how many verses each student memorized, and then bill the adult sponsors accordingly.

Either way, your kids will have not just money in their pockets, but the words of life in their hearts! *Greg Pile and John Stumbo*

LAWN-A-THON

Promise free lawn mowing, and still raise youth group funds! Line up as many kids as you can with lawn mowers, and provide transportation for each of them. Advertise with fliers and posters that on a certain Saturday, your group will mow lawns for free. Get as many people as you can to sign up to have their lawn mowed.

Now, for the money-making part. Pass out pledge sheets to all of your teens and have them get people to pledge 10 cents, 20 cents, or whatever for each lawn that your group mows from 6:00 a.m. to 6:00 p.m. that day. This not only raises money for your group, but also provides a real service to people in your community. *Rick Wheeler*

CAR WASH-A-THON

Here's a different way to make sure your next car wash is a big success. However, since it does involve people donating money as opposed to actually buying a car wash, it is best to reserve this for raising funds for the needy, as opposed to raising money to send the youth group to a theme park.

Basically the way it works is this: In addition to selling car wash tickets, you take pledges for the number of cars washed during the day—not just how many one person washes, but the group as a whole. In other words, if someone pledged 10 cents per car washed, and during the day the group washed a total of 70 cars, that would be $7. If each gets $1 to $2 in pledges, as well as their car wash tickets, it adds up to very good income for a regular old car wash.

As with any car wash make sure that plenty of kids are on hand to do the washing. Be sure there are plenty of hoses, towels, buckets, chamois, scrub brushes, vacuum cleaners, etc. Also make sure each car is washed better than the automatic car wash down the street. It will make things easier when it comes time to promote the next car wash. *Bill Rudge*

READ-A-THON

A similar activity is a Bible-a-Thon, but the Read-a-Thon is a little more flexible. The idea is simply to choose a weekend or other convenient time for continuous reading—from the Bible, Christian literature, or other good literature—for as long as possible.

One group did this beginning on a Friday afternoon and read from the Bible non-stop until Sunday morning service. One person would read while everyone else in the group sat in the audience and followed along. The readers would switch off during the entire time, each reading for as long as he or she could. The group was able to read all of Genesis, Exodus, Joshua, Judges, Ruth, 1 and 2 Samuel, 1 and 2 Kings, Job, Psalms, Proverbs, Ecclesiastes, Song of Solomon, Isaiah, Jonah, Daniel, Matthew, John, Acts, Romans, 1 and 2 Corinthians, Galatians, Ephesians, Philippians, 1 and 2 John, and Revelation.

Each kid obtains sponsors who pledge a certain amount for each hour of continuous reading. This can raise a pretty good sum if the kids work at it. For example, 30 kids getting about $5 per hour in pledges can raise $3,600 for one 24-hour day. But what makes this fundraiser really different is that you can also arrange to have someone record the entire Read-a-Thon on cassette tapes. These tapes can then be used to provide either the Bible or other literature to elderly people who find it difficult to read or to the blind. Recording also helps ensure that the kids will read without messing up too much.

The advantage to reading something other than Scripture is the danger of kids getting so sick of reading the Bible after this ordeal, that they never pick it up again. So you might consider reading C.S. Lewis, Tolkien, or other good literature that kids can learn from as well as enjoy. But the Bible can be used so long as the experience is a good one, a lot of fun, and

not forced upon anyone. Be sure and give kids periodic breaks—five minutes per hour—to eat, stretch, go to the bathroom, and so on. Also have the kids get plenty of rest before the event, and allow anyone to quit whenever they want to. *William C. Humphries*

IRONMAN CONTEST

Select some willing male church board and staff members or dads to compete in this hilarious fund-raiser. The contestants—armed with their own irons, ironing boards, and shirts—will iron as many shirts as possible in a given amount of time. Each shirt is judged for quality and detail while people in the audience pledge money to any or all of the Ironmen for each shirt completed. A trophy is presented to the best overall Ironman—though all contestants receive certificates. See the Ironman Contest certificate on page 117. Collect pledge money before the event ends.

• **Promotion.** A few weeks before the contest, perform a skit for the congregation, playing off the idea of the Ironman Triathlon. The Ironman Promotional Dialogue is on page 117. Another Sunday invite to the front one of the contestants who's claiming to be the shoe-in winner and have him show off a shirt he has been practicing on. It should be burned clear through in places and scorched in others.

• **Refreshments.** Line up several of the best cooks to make their favorite dessert bar to bring the night of the contest. The youth group can provide drinks for everyone.

• **The Trophy.** Make an Ironman trophy. At any trophy shop purchase a marble base ($4-$7) with an undated brass plate engraved with the words IRONMAN CHAMPION.

Then find an old travel iron at a thrift shop, spray it with gold paint, and mount it on the base. You can circulate the trophy in subsequent Ironman fund-raisers.

• **The Pledges.** Take pledges the night of the contest to save time and planning. Or you can display pictures of the contestants in a high-traffic area of your church and let your youths collect pledges in advance for any or all of the Ironmen. See the Ironman Pledge Sheet on page 118.

• **The Big Day.** Set up the contest like a TV game show. Ask someone to keep a hilarious running commentary on the contestants during the action. Use a portable scoreboard clock or videotape a scoreboard/swimming clock and play the tape to show the time elapsed. Play some fast-paced game show music to intensify the contest. Contestants' wives can act as personal trainers and coaches. Give them water bottles and sweat rags and let them play their part to the hilt.

• **Judging.** Have judges use the Ironman Contest Judging Form (page 119) to determine the winner of the contest. Check for things like creases on the sleeves, wrinkles in the collar, smoothness around the buttons, pleats in the back, overall crispness of the shirt, whether an apron was worn, whether the wife helped. Each area is rated from one to 10.

• **The Conspiracy.** Midway through the contest, draw the audience's attention to the fact that the trophy is missing and accuse one of the contestants of stealing the trophy and selling it. Then, on a TV in the room, play a hidden-camera video (like FBI footage) of two unidentified people in a motel room exchanging the trophy for a large sum of money.

Presentation is everything for the Ironman Contest to be successful. Make it fun for the audience as well as for the contestants. Have plenty of pledge sheets on hand so that everyone present can get in on the fun. *Martin Barker*

TRASH-A-THON

One problem with most -a-Thons is that they accomplish little or nothing in themselves except raising money. The Trash-a-Thon, however, strikes a blow for a better environment as it makes the bucks. Instead of sitting in a rocking chair, taking a hike, or riding a bike, the kids pick up litter. They get people to sponsor them for a given amount of money for each large trash bag full of litter they pick up.

Selecting a nice dirty spot is key. Your city or county health or pollution department may be able to help you find the worst spot, which in this case is the best. If the spot is good and cruddy, each kid can pick up 15 to 20 bags in about five hours with no sweat. This project appeals to sponsors because they are helping clean up their town as well as helping your kids. You may be able to talk to a local merchant into providing a couple of prizes for your kids—like one prize for the kid with the most sponsors and another for the kid who picks up the most trash. *Ray Houser*

DOMINO DROP

Many have seen the incredible domino mazes in which dominoes are placed end to end in a huge design. Then the domino at the beginning of the design is pushed

Ironman Promotional Dialogue

Perform this promotional skit to your congregation a week or two before the Ironman Contest. Equip someone with a ridiculous amount of athletic gear—bike, biker's helmet, running shoes, Lycra tights, stopwatch, etc. Throw in a snorkel, mask, and backpack.

PERSON is already in the auditorium. IRONMAN enters.

PERSON: *(as if Ironman is interrupting)* Excuse me!
IRONMAN: Huh?
PERSON: Who are you?
IRONMAN: Biff.
PERSON: What are you doing, Biff?
IRONMAN: Radical mind twister, dude. I'm training.
PERSON: Training for what?
IRONMAN: The greatest test of man's endurance, agility, and strength.
PERSON: And what might that be?
IRONMAN: The Ironman Contest, man. See my equipment?
PERSON: Yeah...that's, uh, impressive...but isn't the Ironman Triathlon in Hawaii?
IRONMAN: No, man. I just saw posters up everywhere saying there's gonna be an Ironman Contest here.
PERSON: Well, yes. We are having an Ironman Contest, but it's not the same kind of Ironman Contest.
IRONMAN: Huh?
PERSON: Want to see the trophy? *(holds up trophy of an iron—as in "ironing board")*
IRONMAN: Dude! That's an iron!
PERSON: Very perceptive! Our Ironman Contest will decide which of our Ironmen from our church board are the best at "pressing" toward their goal of being the best at handling an iron. It's to help raise money for the youth department here at _____ *(name of your church)*.
IRONMAN: Totally excellent! But what about food? I'm not coming unless there's food.
PERSON: We'll have some of the best desserts that you'll find anywhere. It all happens here _____ *(date and time)*, so don't miss it.

IRONMAN
C O N T E S T

This is to certify that

_____

participated in the
19____ IRONMAN Contest
and has received the

_____

award on this

_____ day of _____, 19____

117

IRONMAN
PLEDGE SHEET

Name: _____

Address:_____

City: _____

Zip: _____ Phone: _____

Please fill out your pledge by indicating which Ironman you would like to pledge towards.
1. Write in the amount you want to pledge per shirt.
2. When the contest is finished, calculate what the total is for each Ironman.
3. Add up your total for all pledges taken.
4. When you have completed your form, take it to the designated table where you can arrange for payment.
5. The stub at the bottom of this form can be used as a receipt.

Ironmen	Pledges per shirt	Total pledged
_____	$___per shirt (x___shirts)	= $_____
_____	$___per shirt (x___shirts)	= $_____
_____	$___per shirt (x___shirts)	= $_____
_____	$___per shirt (x___shirts)	= $_____
_____	$___per shirt (x___shirts)	= $_____
_____	$___per shirt (x___shirts)	= $_____

GRAND TOTAL $ _____

- -

Thank you for your continuing support for the youth department.

IRONMAN Contest

_____
(date)

Thank you for your support! Total $_____

IRONMAN
JUDGING FORM

for _____
(contestant's name)

Rate each category on a scale from 1 to 10

____ Completed shirt

____ Wore apron

____ Creases on sleeves

____ Collar

____ Button front

____ Overall crispness of shirt

____ No help from wife

_____ **Total**

IRONMAN
JUDGING FORM

for _____
(contestant's name)

Rate each category on a scale from 1 to 10

____ Completed shirt

____ Wore apron

____ Creases on sleeves

____ Collar

____ Button front

____ Overall crispness of shirt

____ No help from wife

_____ **Total**

over and one by one all the others fall until the entire maze collapses. Many of these designs are so intricate that it takes many minutes for all the dominoes to fall.

Have your youth group get people to pledge a certain amount of money per domino. Then have your group design a pattern of dominoes that will include as many dominoes as they can get their hands on. They, of course, practice ahead of time to find the best design possible. When they have finished their final design, they push the first domino and watch them all fall. Count all the fallen dominoes, and then multiply by the pledge for each domino. This can be a novel fundraiser and a lot of fun for everyone involved. *Bob Moyer*

OTHER FUNDRAISING IDEAS

PUSHBALL MARATHON

Obtain a giant pushball and plan a day during which your youths will push it all over the community, up and down streets for a distance of from five to 25 miles or so. You may have to obtain a parade permit in your city depending on the conditions, so check this out. Have the kids take pledges from adults to give them so much a mile to push the ball. Pledges may range from five cents to five dollars per mile. The money can be used for a worthy project or charity in the community and, with a little advertising, can be a very successful service project. Have a car or van with a sign on it lead the way, so that onlookers know what's going on. *Steve Riggle*

BOOK BLAST

Have the youth group write a book. Really tap the creative potential of the group and have the kids write stories, poetry, articles and essays or submit cartoons, drawings, and anything else that can be reproduced. Then have it all edited by a committee, pasted up, and printed by the offset process. (Photos can be included this way.) Or do the whole thing on your PC. A local printer or bindery can bind them into books. Select a catchy title and design a nice cover which can be printed on cover stock. The books can then be advertised and sold in the church and community as a fine fundraising project. *Mary McKemy*

VINTAGE T-SHIRT AUCTION

If you or your predecessors used T-shirts for camps, retreats, and special events, there's probably a pile of vintage T-shirts stuck away in some closet in the youth department. Don't use them as rags for the car wash or merely give them away. Sell 'em!

Advertise the auction with the antiquity of the shirts (T-shirts Dating Back as Far as 1972!). If you have no especially old ones, confiscate an old college T-shirt from one of your sponsors and surprise the kids with it. Start the bidding and watch the fun as the young people buy replacements for their own T-shirt collections, shirts from events they never heard of, and shirts for their teddy bears. *R. Michael Naron*

HUBCAP OFFERING PLATES

Tired of formal offering plates? Add a little class to your youth group meetings by using hubcaps for offering plates. Most auto junk yards are willing to donate a couple for a good cause. Choose bowl-shaped hubcaps, and line them with velvet or felt. Put them to use between meetings as wall hangings. *Bob King*

HELIUM BALLOONS

Your group can make money on Valentine's Day or any other special day by selling and delivering helium balloons. Have kids take orders three weeks prior to the holiday, and then make arrangements with a local balloon or stationery store to supply the balloons and helium at wholesale prices—or maybe even at cost.

Each person ordering a balloon should fill out an order card with name, address, and phone number of the balloon recipient. Include also the seller's name and number of balloons sold. Leave a space on the other side of the card for a message from the sender to the recipient. The customer then pays for the balloon and returns the card to the seller. Collect all cards several days before the special day, and group them by geographic areas.

On delivery day, two people can come early to fill the balloons and attach the messages. The rest of the group can show up about an hour later to deliver them. *Diane E. Deming*

GOLF TOURNAMENT

Some youth programs have had good success with sponsoring golf tournaments in the community. This works best if you are in a large church with a lot of golfers in it or if you have a way of attracting golfers from all over the area.

You will need to reserve a local golf course and work out a deal on green fees if possible. Someone with some golf tournament experience will need to organize the tournament itself, establishing the rules, the tee-off times, and so forth. You can line up some nice donated prizes for the lowest score, highest score, closest to the pin on the 18th hole, etc.

You might want to enlist some celebrity-type players to host each foursome. The entry fee can be high enough to make it a good fundraiser, but low enough to attract lots of players. You can wrap up the tournament with a banquet for presentation of the awards and explanation of the mission.

BULLISH ON THE YOUTH GROUP

Here's an unusual way to finance your next service project. Print up stock certificates and sell them to members of the church or community as an investment. Each share can sell for one dollar with no limit on how many shares a person can buy. Some may want to only buy one share, but others may want to buy a hundred shares. The stock gives them ownership in the project and entitles them to attend a stockholders' meeting so that they can find out how their investment is doing. A stockholders' report can also be printed. Both the meeting and the report can include photos, testimonies by the kids who participated, a financial statement, and so on. *Nancy Freyer*

MONEY MANIA

Want your youth to be obsessed with giving? Try "Money Mania" at your next week of camp or Vacation Bible School. Ask everyone to bring a certain kind of coin each day or night you take up an offering, according to the following plan:

- **Monday.** "Dime Night." Each person gives one dime for every member of his or her family.
- **Tuesday.** "Nickel Night." One nickel for every letter in the giver's name.
- **Wednesday.** "Penny Night." One penny for every pound the giver weighs.
- **Thursday.** "Quarter Night." One quarter for every foot of the giver's height.
- **Friday.** "Dollar Night." One dollar for each heart the giver has!

You can use this system to raise an offering for practically any need. One variation is to take the offerings every Sunday for five weeks. Make sure you have plenty of coin wrappers. You'll be surprised at how much everyone will enjoy giving this way. *Tommy Baker*

BUCKS FOR POINTS

Here's how you can divvy up money from a group fundraiser into the accounts of each participating student.

The operative word is participating. With a point system like that below, students earn credits toward the cost of church-sponsored youth function. The money may even be transferred to another student's account, if student and parents are willing. To arrive at the dollar value of a point, simply divide the total profit of the fundraiser by the total number of points issued.

Say your fundraiser was an enchilada dinner. Early in the planning process, you'd post a chart like the one shown here.

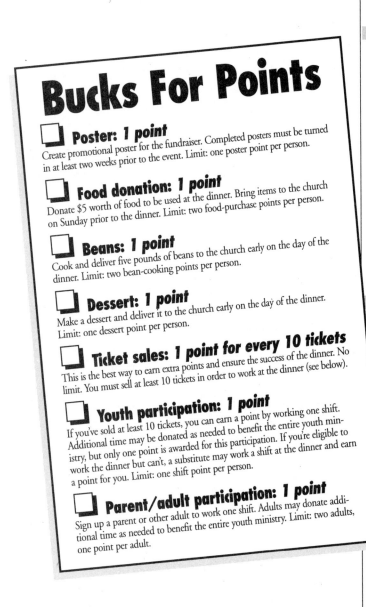

Bucks For Points

☐ **Poster: 1 point**
Create promotional poster for the fundraiser. Completed posters must be turned in at least two weeks prior to the event. Limit: one poster point per person.

☐ **Food donation: 1 point**
Donate $5 worth of food to be used at the dinner. Bring items to the church on Sunday prior to the dinner. Limit: two food-purchase points per person.

☐ **Beans: 1 point**
Cook and deliver five pounds of beans to the church early on the day of the dinner. Limit: two bean-cooking points per person.

☐ **Dessert: 1 point**
Make a dessert and deliver it to the church early on the day of the dinner. Limit: one dessert point per person.

☐ **Ticket sales: 1 point for every 10 tickets**
This is the best way to earn extra points and ensure the success of the dinner. No limit. You must sell at least 10 tickets in order to work at the dinner (see below).

☐ **Youth participation: 1 point**
If you've sold at least 10 tickets, you can earn a point by working one shift. Additional time may be donated as needed to benefit the entire youth ministry, but only one point is awarded for this participation. If you're eligible to work the dinner but can't, a substitute may work a shift at the dinner and earn a point for you. Limit: one shift point per person.

☐ **Parent/adult participation: 1 point**
Sign up a parent or other adult to work one shift. Adults may donate additional time as needed to benefit the entire youth ministry. Limit: two adults, one point per adult.

BUSINESS CARD PLACE MATS

Here's a twist on the pancake breakfast idea that really makes some money. Make up a master place mat for use at the breakfast. On the mat, draw space for a business card. Have youth group members take copies of the master along with a letter of explanation to local businesses and sell the space for advertising. Charge $50 or whatever businesses in your community will support. The space can be filled with the business's card, a small display ad, or something you provide. Several master place mats can be designed, each featuring a different advertiser. Or you can charge each advertiser less and place several advertisements on each place mat. By making copies of the masters, you will have place mats for several church events. *Jeff Keas*

BATTLE OF THE SEXES

Build a wooden balance that will hold two empty paint buckets. Let the girls in the youth group decorate their bucket and the guys decorate theirs. Cut slits in the lids and encourage people in the congregation to drop pocket change into the bucket of their choice. After a predetermined number of Sundays has passed, declare either the heaviest bucket or the one with the most money the winner. If the guys win, the girls wear baseball hats and serve donuts and coffee after church the next week. If the girls win, the guys don aprons and serve sweet rolls and coffee. Adult men and women donate the goodies, and ultimately everyone wins. *Kimberlee Ingraham*

PAPER BOOSTER CLUB

In most areas it is possible to earn money by recycling used newspapers. It takes a lot of paper to make it profitable, but if organized properly, it can be a good way to raise dollars for your ongoing projects.

Enlist the congregation and neighbors to become members of the Paper Boosters Club. When they join you can give them an official membership certificate with the details about pickups. They promise to save all their newspapers especially for your group. Then once a month set up a paper collection route so that your teens can pick up all the paper. If enough people get involved, you can earn a lot of money. The same can be done with aluminum cans and other items that can be recycled for cash. *Dallas Elder*

Youth Ministry Gift Certificates

Events cost money. So to ease the demand on parents for cash, offer gift certificates that can be cashed in for youth group events. Friends, relatives, and neighbors can buy them for birthdays, good grades, bad days, etc. The youth office or church office does the record keeping, and the kids—or their parents—have to come up with less cash out-of-pocket when an event arrives. *Beth Brittain*

Buy-a-Share Fundraiser

Here's how you can raise funds for a mission trip and enlist adults' prayer support as well. During a special youth service, have the members of your team demonstrate the skills they'll use on the mission trip—singing, teaching children's lessons, giving their testimonies, etc. Have them also share the amount of financial assistance they require to participate in the trip.

Meanwhile, out in the church lobby, set up a display your group made beforehand. On the display should be a list of the students going on the mission trip, envelopes bearing the names of the kids, and instructions for the congregation's adults: every envelope represents a $20 share (adjust the share amount to fit your situation). For example, if Tina still needs $80, then four envelopes bear her name. After the service an adult may "buy" a share of Tina by taking an envelope off the display, putting a check or cash for $20 in it, and placing it in the collection plate during the next service.

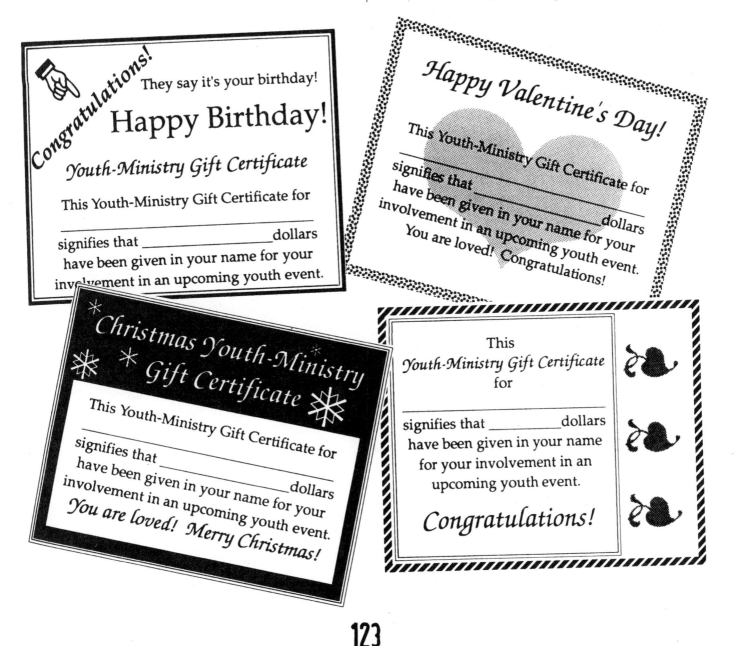

Congratulations! They say it's your birthday!
Happy Birthday!
Youth-Ministry Gift Certificate

This Youth-Ministry Gift Certificate for

_____
signifies that _____ dollars
have been given in your name for your
involvement in an upcoming youth event.

Happy Valentine's Day!

This Youth-Ministry Gift Certificate for
_____
signifies that _____
have been given in your name for your _____ dollars
involvement in an upcoming youth event.
You are loved! Congratulations!

Christmas Youth-Ministry Gift Certificate

This Youth-Ministry Gift Certificate for
_____
signifies that _____
have been given in your name for your _____ dollars
involvement in an upcoming youth event.
You are loved! Merry Christmas!

This
Youth-Ministry Gift Certificate for
_____
signifies that _____ dollars
have been given in your name
for your involvement in an
upcoming youth event.

Congratulations!

Also on the display should be a reminder that buying a share of a teenager commits adults to being their teens' prayer partners before the trip and praying for them during the trip. *Steve Smoker*

NO-SHOW BALL

That's right—you can *not* throw a party that people will pay *not* to come to! Just print formal invitations like the one shown, and mail them throughout the congregation.

The Youth Group
Requests the Pleasure of Your Company
at the

First Annual
No-Show Ball

To Benefit Our
Summer Retreat.
This Ball Is Not To Be Held
on Friday, the Second of June,
Nowhere at All
at No Time Whatsoever,
So Please Don't Come.

RSVP. for The First Church Youth Group

☐ Count on me! Here's my contribution for the new outfit I don't intend to buy.

☐ I won't need to visit the barber or hair stylist, so here's my contribution that I would've paid them. My nonexistent hair appointment is at _____ A.M./P.M.

☐ Thank you for inviting me. I would be glad not to come so that the youth ministry can receive funds to help with its Summer Retreat.

The idea is simple: don't show up, don't dress up, don't get a baby-sitter, don't buy a new outfit, don't have your hair done. And as for any ball they'd attend, you ask them to make a donation. And they do! *Tim Falk*

BIGGER AND BETTER SCAVENGER HUNT

Here's a fundraising version of a scavenger hunt. Divide your group into teams and give each team a penny. Set a time limit, tell the teams what modest prize the winners will get, and then start the event. Each team goes door-to-door throughout the neighborhood, informing residents that they are members of the First Church youth group and are raising money for this or that. Then they say, "May I trade you this penny for something bigger and better?" Teams will probably receive a nickel, dime, or quarter for the penny, which at the next house they attempt to trade up. This continues until the original penny becomes a dollar—then teams start over with a penny again.

It's surprising how much your group can make in only an hour. And there are other advantages: no complicated planning is required for this fundraiser, your teenagers see money coming in immediately, large donations are not required, and it's an excellent opportunity to establish a name for yourselves in the community. *Kerry Glenn*

RADIO DAY

Make an appointment with the general manager of a local radio station—Christian or otherwise—and request permission to let your youth group kids sell commercial time. Then air the ads during the afternoon that they are guest DJs. In effect, the radio station will donate commercial time—and the income derived from those commercials—to your group.

Here are the details: Find a business—perhaps a Christian bookstore—in which you can set up a remote broadcast for four hours. Charge them less than a radio station would for the publicity they'll receive all afternoon on the broadcast, for an interview or two with the owner or manager of the business, and for the pre-event publicity they'll receive in newspaper and television public-service announcements.

Radio stations will either give you free air time or charge you per hour. They will probably let your DJs read commercials from the businesses that buy advertising, while the actual DJ plays the music at the radio station.

About selling advertising: Collect the names and addresses of businesses your church does consistent business with, of Christian-owned business-es, of church members who own businesses, etc. Divide the list up among your young people, write a script like the sample given that they can follow as they talk to businesses and sell them commercial time. Treat these teen telemarketers to lunch the last day of the selling period. The sponsors or youth workers of some groups make follow-up calls to each business that bought air time, in order to dou-ble-check the information—especially the actual ad that the business wants read over the air. If a business doesn't provide its own written ad, a cre-ative student or you will have to write it.

Obtain a time clock (see diagram) from the station's program director, and number your com-mercials with the corresponding number at the time they are to be read. Organize your student DJs into shifts, rotating every hour or two.

A week before the broadcast, tell your television stations and newspapers what you're doing. They're usually glad to show up, shoot some frames or footage, and do a public-service announcement or a feature write-up. *Rick Bowles*

Church Youth Radio Day
on WBCT

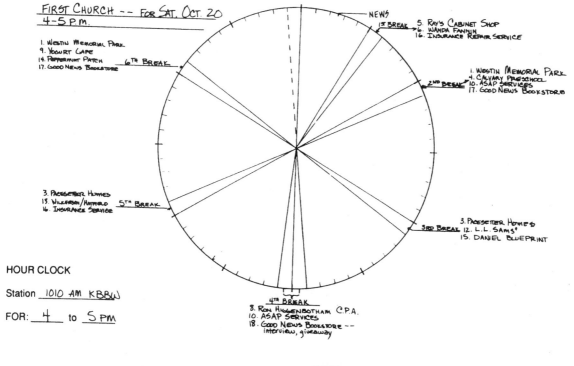

YELLOW PAGE DIRECTORIES

Your group can raise money by publishing its own Yellow Pages to sell to church members. Sell individual business listings in the directory for five to ten dollars each to local merchants and professionals, especially those in the church. In addition, the youth can include their own listings for yard work, baby-sitting, and other jobs.

Try to compile the whole thing on computer so that it can easily be updated for future use. Create categories of businesses and alphabetize the names of specific businesses within each category. Let the kids work on this with adult supervision. You can charge extra for offering businesses the opportunity to call more attention to their listings with larger type or bold type or boxed type. Directories can be sold for a dollar or more to church members, providing them with a useful service as well as raising funds for your program. *Rosalind Rodes*

PERPETUAL RECYCLING FUNDRAISER

Do you live in a state or city where empty bottles and cans have a recycling value? Then start an ongoing fundraiser that frees you to spend more time ministering to kids.

Set up a big cardboard box—like a large appliance box—or a simple plywood box somewhere in the church, and decorate it with wrapping paper. Announce to the congregation that the youth group is starting a nonstop fundraiser collecting returnable bottles and cans. Be sure you let parishioners know exactly where the drop box is.

And when you're ready to take the bottles and cans to the recycler, invite one or two kids to go along with you. *Bill Kingsley*

30 PIECES OF SILVER

At Easter time, an effective way to receive a special offering from your youth for a worthwhile project would be to have everyone bring a plastic sandwich bag with 30 pieces of silver in it. Any denomination of coin is acceptable, so long as it is silver. *Jim Scott*

TEATIME FUNDRAISER

Sometimes people get tired of youth groups selling tickets or going to fundraising banquets, car washes, bake sales, etc. So here's a different approach. Mail each church member a letter stating, "We know you are tired of fundraisers, offering pitches, etc...so sit back, take off your shoes, relax, and have a cup of tea on us." In each envelope you place a tea bag. Also ask the church member, "While you are relaxing, we'd like you to think about your youth group and consider helping them with their special project...(etc.)." Casually ask for a donation, but make it as soft a sell as possible. One group raised $800 with this approach and got many compliments. *Patsy Quested*

PENNY DRIVE

The penny drive is a fundraiser that encourages maximum involvement from both your youth group and congregation and the rewards are worth it. Much money can be raised and worthwhile projects can be accomplished with just pennies.

Get your senior high group to set a date and advertise only to the congregation. The project should be a one-day event from 9:00 a.m. to 5:00 p.m. Choose a mission project where the money is to be given and then develop themes and advertising that will be catchy and appealing to all in the church—Windmills for Ethiopia or Kilowatts for Katpadi, for example.

People are notified in advance that the pennies are to be brought to the church on the specified day only. When people bring their pennies, have your youth group there to take the pennies and place them on a large picture cut out of white paper, which should be placed on the floor. As the pennies are placed on the picture, an effective mosaic-like design begins to form. People will come back all day long to watch how the design is progressing.

If people come with checks or dollar bills, have pennies on hand for exchange. Simply go to a bank for a supply. Once this event becomes a tradition, people will start saving pennies all year long in anticipation of the penny drive. *Dick Vriesman*

126

CALENDAR PAYOFF

Encourage your teens to be givers. Print up a calendar that has a space for each day of the month. In each space, enter an instruction that will determine how much money they must give that day. The instruction should be humorous and vary the amount given from one day to the next. When the month is up, the kids bring in the money they owe. At that time you can give awards for who had to pay the most money, the least, the most expensive day of the month, etc.

A variation of this payoff would be to print the instruction for each day on separate sheets of paper, fold and staple them, so they are concealed until the end of each day. The instruction can then be a fine for certain things done or not done. For example, it might say "Pay five cents for each class you were late to today," or "Pay 25 cents if you forgot to brush your teeth," etc.

Allow a space on the calendar where kids can write in how much they owe each day. They can just total it up at the end of the month. You might add one extra space for them to give any amount they choose. This approach adds a little fun and variety to giving. *Dallas Elder*

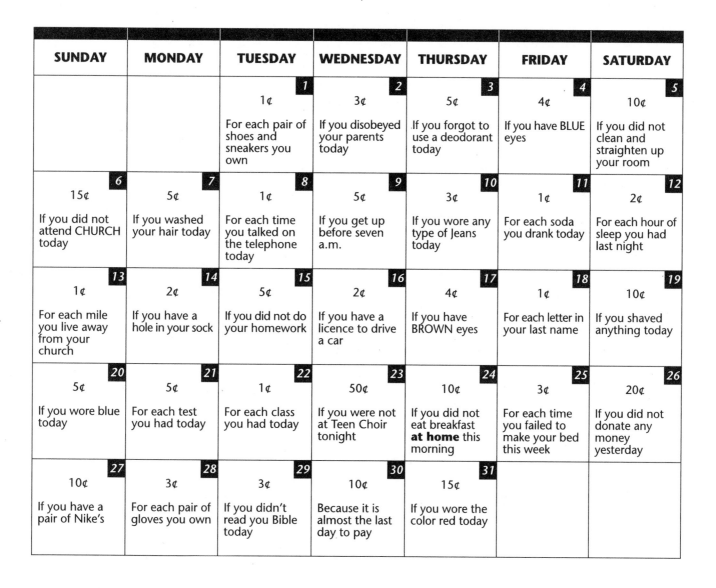

SUNDAY	MONDAY	TUESDAY	WEDNESDAY	THURSDAY	FRIDAY	SATURDAY
		1 1¢ For each pair of shoes and sneakers you own	**2** 3¢ If you disobeyed your parents today	**3** 5¢ If you forgot to use a deodorant today	**4** 4¢ If you have BLUE eyes	**5** 10¢ If you did not clean and straighten up your room
6 15¢ If you did not attend CHURCH today	**7** 5¢ If you washed your hair today	**8** 1¢ For each time you talked on the telephone today	**9** 5¢ If you get up before seven a.m.	**10** 3¢ If you wore any type of Jeans today	**11** 1¢ For each soda you drank today	**12** 2¢ For each hour of sleep you had last night
13 1¢ For each mile you live away from your church	**14** 2¢ If you have a hole in your sock	**15** 5¢ If you did not do your homework	**16** 2¢ If you have a licence to drive a car	**17** 4¢ If you have BROWN eyes	**18** 1¢ For each letter in your last name	**19** 10¢ If you shaved anything today
20 5¢ If you wore blue today	**21** 5¢ For each test you had today	**22** 1¢ For each class you had today	**23** 50¢ If you were not at Teen Choir tonight	**24** 10¢ If you did not eat breakfast **at home** this morning	**25** 3¢ For each time you failed to make your bed this week	**26** 20¢ If you did not donate any money yesterday
27 10¢ If you have a pair of Nike's	**28** 3¢ For each pair of gloves you own	**29** 3¢ If you didn't read you Bible today	**30** 10¢ Because it is almost the last day to pay	**31** 15¢ If you wore the color red today		

YOUTH SPECIALTIES TITLES

Professional Resources

Administration, Publicity, & Fundraising (Ideas Library)

Developing Student Leaders

Equipped to Serve: Volunteer Youth Worker Training Course

Help! I'm a Junior High Youth Worker!

Help! I'm a Sunday School Teacher!

Help! I'm a Volunteer Youth Worker!

How to Expand Your Youth Ministry

How to Speak to Youth...and Keep Them Awake at the Same Time

One Kid at a Time: Reaching Youth through Mentoring

A Youth Ministry Crash Course

The Youth Worker's Handbook to Family Ministry

Youth Ministry Programming

Camps, Retreats, Missions, & Service Ideas (Ideas Library)

Compassionate Kids: Practical Ways to Involve Your Students in Mission and Service

Creative Bible Lessons in John: Encounters with Jesus

Creative Bible Lessons in Romans: Faith on Fire!

Creative Bible Lessons on the Life of Christ

Creative Junior High Programs from A to Z, Vol. 1 (A-M)

Creative Meetings, Bible Lessons, & Worship Ideas (Ideas Library)

Crowd Breakers & Mixers (Ideas Library)

Drama, Skits, & Sketches (Ideas Library)

Dramatic Pauses

Facing Your Future: Graduating Youth Group with a Faith That Lasts

Games (Ideas Library)

Games 2 (Ideas Library)

Great Fundraising Ideas for Youth Groups

More Great Fundraising Ideas for Youth Groups

Great Retreats for Youth Groups

Greatest Skits on Earth

Greatest Skits on Earth, Vol. 2

Holiday Ideas (Ideas Library)

Hot Illustrations for Youth Talks

More Hot Illustrations for Youth Talks

Incredible Questionnaires for Youth Ministry

Junior High Game Nights

More Junior High Game Nights

Kickstarters: 101 Ingenious Intros to Just about Any Bible Lesson

Memory Makers

Play It! Great Games for Groups

Play It Again! More Great Games for Groups

Special Events (Ideas Library)

Spontaneous Melodramas

Super Sketches for Youth Ministry

Teaching the Bible Creatively

Up Close and Personal: How to Build Community in Your Youth Group

Wild Truth Bible Lessons

Worship Services for Youth Groups

Discussion Starter Resources

Discussion & Lesson Starters (Ideas Library)

Discussion & Lesson Starters 2 (Ideas Library)

4th-6th Grade TalkSheets

Get 'Em Talking

High School TalkSheets

High School TalkSheets: Psalms and Proverbs

Junior High TalkSheets

Junior High TalkSheets: Psalms and Proverbs

Keep 'Em Talking!

More High School TalkSheets

More Junior High TalkSheets

Parent Ministry TalkSheets

What If...? 450 Thought-Provoking Questions to Get Teenagers Talking, Laughing, and Thinking

Would You Rather...? 465 Provocative Questions to Get Teenagers Talking

Clip Art

ArtSource Vol. 1—Fantastic Activities

ArtSource Vol. 2—Borders, Symbols, Holidays, and   Attention Getters

ArtSource Vol. 3—Sports

ArtSource Vol. 4—Phrases and Verses

ArtSource Vol. 5—Amazing Oddities and Appalling Images

ArtSource Vol. 6—Spiritual Topics

ArtSource Vol. 7—Variety Pack

ArtSource Vol. 8—Stark Raving Clip Art

ArtSource CD-ROM (contains Vols. 1-7)

Videos

EdgeTV

The Heart of Youth Ministry: A Morning with Mike Yaconelli

Next Time I Fall in Love Video Curriculum

Understanding Your Teenager Video Curriculum

Student Books

Grow For It Journal

Grow For It Journal through the Scriptures

Wild Truth Journal for Junior Highers